AF409800

LOVE YOURSELF

30 days

to learn to love yourself

Daniel J. Martin

ISBN 978-9916-9938-3-5

Disclaimer: This book has been created with the intention of providing information, suggestions, and guidance on various areas of life, including emotional well-being, mental health, personal growth, and the development of healthy relationships. However, it does not substitute for professional medical care or the advice of a qualified psychologist or therapist. If you are facing serious mental or emotional health issues, we recommend you seek professional help immediately.

*"Love yourself first and everything else
falls into line."*

— Lucille Ball

CONTENTS

DOWNLOAD THE AUDIOBOOK FREE!

*If you would rather enjoy **Love Yourself** on the go, you can download its audio version completely FREE!*

www.danieljmartin.es/audio/lys

The "Love Yourself More" method

We've all heard how important it is to love ourselves, and that healthy self-esteem can be the difference between being a happy, successful person and not being one.

But when it comes to putting it into practice, most methods and techniques for boosting self-esteem are an utter failure. Many people who decide to work on their self-worth – with the mental and emotional effort that involves – end up carrying the same baggage year after year, seeing little to no improvement. The sad truth is that so many people will dedicate their entire lives to fighting to feel better about themselves without ever managing it.

So, why does this happen?

Simply put, it's about the method. If the method is faulty, it doesn't matter how well you execute it.

Self-esteem as a concept is no mystery; on the contrary, it's relatively easy to explain and to grasp. However, it's rarely approached correctly. A good method should first convey the right knowledge in terms of how self-esteem works for an adult and then identify all the areas where someone, not knowing how – or even knowing how – stops trusting themselves, goes from believing they are valid to believing they are a fraud, or thinks they deserve contempt instead of love.

Can you relate? Do you feel that you deserve more (more respect, more confidence, more recognition, more love) but don't know where to get it from? Do you believe your current occupation is beneath you? Do you suffer from stress or anxiety? Do you think it's unfair that someone with fewer virtues than you might achieve more or be happier? Do you find it hard to set boundaries? What about asking for help when you need it? Do you constantly put yourself down for no reason? Do you find it hard to accept and love yourself?

Answering yes to the above questions is a clear sign of low self-esteem. The bad news is that self-love doesn't emerge out of nowhere from one day to the next; the good news is that, if you work on it **in the right way**, self-love grows, feeds into itself and shines its light into every other aspect of your life.

You can build good self-esteem at any age and in any situation, but it's not easy to change the dynamics and beliefs that you've been holding onto for so long. That's why a good method is so important.

The "Love Yourself More" method

What I teach in this book, my proven method for improving your self-esteem in 30 days, is not just "my opinion": **it's science**. This book is based on psychology studies and knowledge, on a science rooted in data, observation of reality, hypotheses and verified results. Because of this, and because it's led to extraordinary results for hundreds of patients of mine, I know that the method I'm proposing to you works.

If you've read this far, don't stop now: **all you need is 30 days and a desire to fulfil your dreams and goals**.

So, why 30 days?

I decided to make this book a thirty-day read because I see it as a kind of bootcamp: intensive training over 30 consecutive days[1]. Each day, I tackle one aspect related to self-esteem, or the lack of it, and suggest a final exercise to put into practice to help you internalize everything you've learned. The thirty-day period is enough to immerse yourself fully, assimilate the concepts and achieve the necessary learning.

Note: Self-esteem is a muscle, and like other muscles, you don't make it bigger by reading books and theory, but by putting it to work. You will need to exercise it.

I'm not your cheerleader or your motivational coffee cup. I'm your personal growth expert and my job is to teach you how to improve your quality of life, and you don't achieve that through a simple "you can do it" or "you're worth more". If you're prepared to take this step with me, I'll be

---

[1] Of course, you can do it in the order you want: read the book in a day, take two months, or begin at the end. But I suggest this structure, because 30 days is the optimum time period to assimilate the concepts and be able to complete the exercises I set you.

by your side, guiding you throughout – but you have to meet me halfway and do your "homework". You should be ready to question your beliefs, change dynamics and make decisions that not everyone will like. It's not easy, but I promise you, it's worth it.

Imagine yourself reaching the goals you've always dreamed of. Imagine yourself feeling at peace with who you are, no matter what. Imagine yourself waking up every morning feeling confident and full of energy, experiencing happiness and joy in every moment of your life...

Now, stop imagining it!

Take that first step and dive into this exciting read. Because in 30 days, your life can change forever.

Daniel

What we mean by self-love

You are the protagonist of the greatest love story you'll ever experience. And do you know who stars opposite you? That's right! You do.

This might sound overly sentimental, but it's true that you are going to live through a love story with yourself, whether you like it or not. It's up to you whether that love story is genuine or fake, intense or superficial. Because, as with all love stories, it's going to knock you down at times, bringing moments of fear, powerlessness, sadness, loneliness. Don't let any of those knocks put out the flame of your love. On the contrary: love your life and your story right to the end, more than anything, and more than ever when you feel unworthy of your own love.

"To love oneself is the beginning of a lifelong romance."

— Oscar Wilde

Nowadays, everyone knows that self-esteem is essential for a full and successful life. However, this knowledge alone doesn't help many people: on the contrary, being aware that they should improve their self-esteem and seeing the years go by without it materializing frustrates and disheartens people even further.

As I said in the introduction, it's usually a problem with the method. All too often, self-esteem issues are approached superficially and "patched up" using techniques that temporarily relieve discomfort without getting to the heart of the matter.

Through my work, I talk to many people who seem to be going through specific troubles (classics like "I don't like my job", "my partner always seems disappointed in me", "I have anxiety") but who, when we go into more depth, uncover a deeper and more serious issue: a lack of self-love.

So, what is exactly is self-love?

Self-love is the fundamental principle that we deserve to be loved by ourselves, now and forever. It's the conviction that we are valid people who are worthy despite our errors and regardless of our abilities.

Self-love is like a gift from life to us. Even if we refuse to open the door to receive it, the gift is out here, whether we accept it or not.

Why wouldn't you accept a gift that will make your life better? What's wrong with receiving love? What's wrong with you?

There is nothing wrong with you. You're not inadequate, nor are you the rehearsal for your "definitive" self, nor do you have too many problems to worry about *loving yourself*. You are a perfectly valid person. In fact, you're an amazing person!

Think about the people who love you, the people who want you to be in the world. About all the times that someone was impressed by something you did. About the people who have kissed or hugged you with sincere affection. About the people who include you in their plans and their lives. Are they all mistaken?

You're an incredible person to lots of people – so why not to yourself?

Find the hero inside you

You know that within you is a hero or heroine waiting to be freed. Loving yourself is the same as freeing that hero inside you.

You are worthy of your love, here and now. Try it. You have nothing to lose by saying: "Alright, challenge accepted: I'm going to try love, let's see if this works!"

Your love story may not be perfect. But, without a doubt, it will be unique. And I promise you: it will be worth it.

Summary:

- Self-love is the fundamental principle that we deserve to be loved by ourselves, now and always.

- Often, the discomfort we feel when faced with work, social or relationship problems is actually low self-esteem.

- Self-esteem is the belief that we are valid people who are worthy regardless of our mistakes or abilities.

- Love yourself in every situation, and love yourself more than ever when you feel unworthy: that's when you need it most.

Daily exercise:

<u>YOU ARE YOUR OWN HERO / HEROINE</u>

1.   Choose five things you like about yourself. Don't be embarrassed or modest: in the same way that you harshly criticize yourself, you need to learn to talk up your positive aspects.

2. Write down those good points in a notebook or on your phone as if they were superpowers. For example: "I have the superpower of being optimistic", "I have the superpower of being respectful with my partner", "I have the superpower of generosity", "I have the superpower of being able to fix devices and objects in record time", "I have the superpower of amazing cooking skills", and so on.

3.   If you look back at your list regularly, you'll soon see that your self-image will improve, and with it, your self-love.

Accept yourself, now and always

We tend to accept the good things we have, but what about the bad? Do we accept them too, or just pretend to, even though deep down they're killing us?

If we only accept the good things we have, we're not accepting ourselves at all. Because acceptance should be of ourselves as a whole, not just what's "easy" or pleasant.

Accepting yourself means admitting that you are vulnerable and imperfect and are still worthy of love, regardless of whether others think that's right and despite the mistakes you may have made.

Accepting yourself is the obligatory first step to loving yourself, and it means accepting your physical self, your past and your limitations.

You might be thinking: "How can I accept all those aspects of myself when I hate them so much?". Well, *accept* doesn't mean *agree with* or *like*; it means come to terms with the fact that right now, that's how it is.

Do you feel unattractive? Has someone treated you badly in the past and made you bitter? Are you envious? I'm guessing all this makes you mad, ashamed, or both. So, how do you accept that?

The first thing is to understand that you don't need to be dazzled by your own looks or forgive that person who deceived you or be happy for what someone else has if, deep down, you're not:

acceptance doesn't mean turning the other cheek! It means refusing to devote the rest of your life to being consumed by something and perpetually blaming yourself for it.

What acceptance is and is not

All this is not me saying that you should lie on the couch and watch life go by just because you love yourself no matter what. Loving and accepting yourself unconditionally does not mean acting spoiled. Just as a mother can tell her child off while still loving and respecting them deeply, you can grow and improve day by day – that's not incompatible with loving yourself right now.

Loving yourself doesn't mean being self-indulgent or having double standards (I don't demand of myself what I demand of others). It means being prepared to construct the best version of yourself with an understanding of your own limitations and those of the world around you, and rejecting any act of violence or contempt toward yourself.

Summary:

–   Accepting yourself is the first step toward building healthy self-esteem.

–   Accepting doesn't mean agreeing with something, it means coming to terms with the way it is.

–   Loving yourself isn't about being self-indulgent, it's about being ready to build the best version of yourself without punishing yourself for your own limitations or those of the world around you.

Daily exercise:

ACCEPTING THE NEGATIVES

1.   Write down on a pad or your phone some mistakes you have made or aspects of yourself that you don't like. For example: "I don't like being so indecisive", "I don't like getting stressed out over small things", "I made a mistake by taking that job", "I think that purchase was a mistake", and so on.

2.   Review your list (you can modify it whenever you want) and, out loud or mentally, repeat an affirmation of self-love after every point. For example: "I made x mistake on x occasion, but that doesn't mean I deny myself my own love. Instead, I'll work on continuing to improve and grow every day."

3.   In time, you'll learn to be fairer with yourself and to separate your mistakes and flaws

from your worth as a person. Remember: you are not your mistakes.

Your body is okay

Humans are the only creatures on earth who spend half their lives ashamed of their own bodies. We feel it even when our bodies have no health issues and are working perfectly normally.

Even then, we don't think we're attractive enough: our legs should be longer, our bellies flatter, our noses smaller, our hair thicker.

I'm not denying that those things can make people more attractive in modern society. They probably can. What I'm saying is that our physical imperfections shouldn't stop us from leading full and loving lives. I mean, would you love your mom more if she were a few inches taller?

It's crazy to spend your life battling against your body just because it's not exactly how you want or doesn't look like the current beauty standard. It has other functions, and those are the ones that should count.

What we call "flaws", nature calls "variation", and it's necessary for the survival of our species.

You weren't there the day you were created

Accepting your body is one of the basic pillars of self-esteem, but man, do we find it hard to reconcile ourselves to our "flaws"! We compare ourselves to our friends, strangers or celebrities and we are never satisfied with *what we got given.*

But the truth is that *what we get given* is not up to us, in essence because we weren't there the day we were created.

The day you were conceived, by which I mean the day that the egg and the sperm met and began the embryonic process, your genetic load was already there. It included your skin type, eye color, ear shape and other aspects that people develop a complex about. No one asked for your opinion, no one asked you how you wanted to look – nature just doesn't work that way.

In adolescence, we begin to criticize every inch of our bodies. But how can you be ashamed of "results" you had nothing to do with? It's like going to work at a company and getting blamed for decisions made by its founders before you were even born. It's crazy!

Your body is the result of millions of years of evolution and combinations of genes. You don't need any more explanation than that. Instead, be thankful for being here and for everything that's okay with your body, which is most of it. Take care of it, so that it lasts you well.

Living at peace with your body

"I certainly can't stand in front of a mirror without trying to improve the way I look – you know, by tucking something in or turning to the side."

Can you relate to this quote? It's from the actress Emma Thompson. She said it in an interview on *The Late Show with Stephen Colbert* in June 2022.

If you're like most people, I bet you also wish you could change a few things when you look in the mirror: a flatter belly, a bigger chest, to be taller... But let me tell you one thing: the people who live at peace with their bodies are not the most attractive people. In fact, believe it or not, there is no direct correlation between beauty and happiness, or beauty and self-love. Read that again: no direct correlation.

People who accept the shape of their bodies are the ones who do so naturally, without covering up, without drama. They are people who don't feel the need to hide their defects or to shout them from the rooftops either, looking for approval from god-knows-who.

Your body is your home and your companion on your journey. Instead of constantly judging it, accept it as part of your team.

Summary:

– Don't blame yourself for the body you have: no one asked you at the time what you wanted it to look like.

– What we call "flaws", nature calls "variation", and it's necessary for the survival of the species.

– You're on this earth for more important things than smoother hair or a shorter stature: your goals, dreams and love should come above what your body looks like.

Daily exercise:

<u>HOW TO MAKE YOUR PEACE WITH THE MIRROR</u>

1. Next time you get undressed, look at yourself in the mirror. Pause over the parts you don't like and get ready to accept them. How can you accept something you hate? Well, because as I've already said, accepting something doesn't mean liking it: it just means respecting what you see.

2. Tell yourself, out loud or in your head: "Here and now, this person is me. These are my arms, my legs, my abdomen, my genitals. I don't like every part, but this is how they are and I accept them because they are the reality".

3. If you repeat this exercise every time you look at yourself naked, you'll notice that the emotions your image generates in you will begin to change: you will identify more closely with

your own body and little by little, your resentment toward it will be reduced.

DAY 4

You are not a stereotype

Did you know that in medieval Japan, young women would dye their teeth black because it was considered sexy? Or that in Ancient Greece, the perfect man had a small penis?

Every era and every culture creates its own beauty ideals, and what is undesirable to us today was irresistible in another time. That's why it's not worth getting upset if your body doesn't conform to the beauty standard or if what you're attracted to doesn't align with what's "desirable": it's normal!

Speaking of attraction, let me tell you about an experiment I like to perform and which began as a hobby. I once went out with my girlfriend and some of her colleagues. We were at a bar and I suggested that we all looked around and said who we thought were the best-looking men and women. The group checked everyone out and the verdict was more or less unanimous in terms of who the most objectively attractive people were. Then, I asked them to choose the person they were most sexually attracted to, whether or not that person met the general standard. And that, my friends, was when the debates began; everyone chose a different person, to the great surprise of the others. Fortunately for me, my girlfriend picked me. Only one person stuck with one of the pretty people from the first round.

What I mean by all this is that our own tastes exist outside stereotypes. It's true that we often agree with certain beauty standards, but the way each person feels it is personal.

There are around six billion adults in this world with all different appearances and tastes: stereotypes are needless boundaries.

What's behind beauty standards?

There's something else about stereotypes: they tend not to be arbitrary or organic. There are interests behind their creation. I'm not just talking about the diet or gym industries, I'm talking about the relationship between beauty and power.

Let me give you an example. In Europe, beauty has been associated with fair skin for centuries. A long time ago, the only people who could keep their skin pale were the aristocracy, because they didn't have to work outside in the sun. This identification came to its most extreme expression from the nineteenth century onward, when fair skin came to be associated with "superior" races, or those presented as the only people worthy of ruling the world.

From 1950 onward, by which time most of the West worked indoors and could protect themselves from the sun, tan skin became popular among the rich, who enjoyed long vacations in the sun or snow: once again, beauty was aligning with the elite. Today, the ideal skin should be free from wrinkles or spots until well past seventy, right when we're being most exposed to pollution and solar radiation.

Is it a coincidence that the beauty ideal is always the opposite of how most people look?

I don't think so. The ideal look is used as a mechanism for social control, reserving it for the minority but making it desirable to everyone else. In this context, feeling at ease with our own bodies is almost an act of rebellion, when it should be the norm!

Always remember: beauty standards are neither innocent nor organic. They are unattainable abstract concepts in real life and they serve to widen the gap between social classes and control the desires of the majority of people.

Make the most of yourself

Almost all professionals in the field of personal growth agree that we should be making the most of ourselves: that is, taking care of ourselves to look as good as possible. This might sound like a contradiction of everything I've said about accepting yourself just the way you are – but it's not.

Making the most of yourself means showing respect for who you are by taking care over your physical appearance. It doesn't mean obsessing over perfection or trying to look like someone you're not. Making the most of yourself is an act of self-affirmation and it says: "I'm not perfect, but I take care over my appearance because it's what my body deserves."

You should adopt the habit of looking after your image as a way to honor yourself. Even on the days when you feel most down or stressed – especially on those days, even – making the most of yourself will make you feel much better. If you don't, you're throwing the door open for defeatism.

The simple act of spending time making the most of yourself helps you to feel better about your own body and it's a very potent way of showing yourself some love.

Summary:

– There are around six billion adults in the world with different appearances and tastes: stereotypes are pointless.

– Beauty standards are used as a mechanism of social control, reserving it for the minority but making it desirable to everyone else.

– Making the most of yourself is a powerful way to show yourself love and respect.

Daily exercise:

MY PHYSICAL CHARMS

1. Everyone, absolutely everyone, has parts of their body they like: a pretty mouth, attractive hands, an interesting gaze, sculpted arms. Locate those parts of your body and note them down somewhere visible. Don't be modest: remember, what might not seem special to you might seem like a real privilege to someone else.

2. Use those parts: if you like your hair, find a hairstyle that suits you. If your legs are nice, wear pants or skirts that look amazing on you. Be a flirt, and instead of telling yourself: "I hate how short I am!", start telling yourself: "Alright, I'm not that tall, but man, my hair is awesome."

3. If you get used to making the most of yourself, you'll soon see more attractive aspects than imperfections on your body and you'll feel much more at ease with the body you have – even the parts you don't like (remember, you don't

have to like everything about yourself in order to
love yourself).

Respect your age

Do you feel under pressure to avoid old age at any cost?

Of all the silly things we do to ourselves, I think that not ageing peacefully is the most irrational of all. And it's not exclusive to our society or time: every era has had a real obsession with slowing down the effects of time. And it's totally pointless.

Do you know why?

Because from the moment we're born, our contract with life begins. There are few things written into that agreement, because we still have our entire lives ahead of us at that point, but there is one clause we cannot break: as long as we are living, we are getting older and we will continue to do so. If we stop getting older, it's because we're dead.

That means that every day you are alive, you are accepting that clause (remember, accept doesn't mean like).

Behind the refusal to get older is often the painful perception that we're not making the most of life as much as we would like to. That's why we try to hit the brakes on time and experience now what we should have experienced before, to see if that satisfies us – but that brings problems for the future, when we will want to experience what we should have today but didn't because we were focused on the past.

Instead of that, let's make the most of what we have left, which is a lot. Let's make our pact with life an impressive one. Let's say: "Of course if I could go back, I would do things differently and do something better with my youth, but the only way to come to this conclusion is to have done things the way I did."

How old are you? Say it out loud! Let everyone know! Remember, all you're doing is complying with the "age clause" in your contract with life.

Refusing to age is perpetual torture. You can subject yourself to extortionate beauty treatments, you can make a fool of yourself by acting your shoe size, you can dress like someone twenty years younger than you, but in the end the result is the same: a pointless ordeal.

Summary:

–   Don't try to experience now what you think you should have experienced in the past: in the future, you'll regret spending the present trying to relive the past.

–   Every day that you're alive, you're holding up your end of your contract with life: getting older is obligatory.

–   To refuse to age is to live in perpetual torment.

Daily exercise:

EVERY COURSE IS APPETIZING

1. Imagine that the various life stages (childhood, adolescence, adulthood, old age) are dishes on a restaurant menu (aperitif, appetizer, main course, dessert).

2. Think about some meals you love and that correspond to the different categories on the menu. Relate your favorite dishes to each stage of your life cycle and build your perfect menu.

3. Mentally savor your life stages, understanding that each one brings different flavors and nuances to your existence and that they all deserve to be sampled and enjoyed with passion. If you get used to doing this exercise regularly, your negative thoughts about the passing of time will lessen.

Stop counting calories and start taking care of your health

Self-care is a fundamental act of self-love. But taking care of your health doesn't mean subjecting yourself to the eternal damnation of hypervigilance and treatments, especially if your body doesn't need them.

I mentioned calories in the title, but I could also be talking about food supplements, fitness apps or alternative therapies such as acupuncture, hypnosis, reiki, plant therapy, aromatherapy, chromotherapy, reflexology, Bach remedies, crystal healing, homeopathy, and so on.

I'm not saying all of that can't be beneficial. What I'm saying is that you're not obligated to do anything that doesn't address a real health issue. Do these therapies make you feel better? Then go ahead! But be selective and set limits, or things will get silly; there will always be something new to try. Every time you check your body and find something you don't like (and this will happen often), you'll think maybe you need to try this alternative therapy or subject yourself to that new treatment.

Your body is your home and your mothership

In the same way I advise you not to get into the endless loop of therapies for everything, I will also ask you not to neglect your body. Your organism keeps you alive and breathing, pumping blood and performing other vital functions. All it asks in exchange is that you take care of it. I think that's a fair deal.

Taking care of your health is your responsibility. Not doing so, and leaving everything in the hands of doctors, fate, or relatives and carers, is not just risky: it also demonstrates a deeply childlike attitude.

You don't need a degree in medicine to maintain basic self-care. In fact, all you need is a little common sense, and it's based on four simple pillars:

1. Watch what you eat.

2. Exercise.

3. Avoid toxic habits and behaviors.

4. Follow your doctor's orders.

That's it! If it's so simple, why do we find it so hard?

I think that one key factor is the lack of a short-term reward for healthy habits. In a society accustomed to instant gratification, eating your greens and getting no immediate results can be frustrating. But the reward for self-care takes a while to come, and it often does so subtly. How can that even compete with a delicious pizza with extra cheese?

So where can we find that motivation?

For many of my patients, and for myself, the key is in accepting that taking care of your health is not rewarding in the short term. You simply do it because your body deserves it, and your future self shouldn't suffer for your irresponsibility today.

If you find this hard, look at it as a long-term investment: you don't want to give up something you want right now, but you'll be glad to enjoy it when you truly need it.

Taking care of your health is one more act of self-love and a display of maturity.

Summary:

– Protecting your health is your responsibility and is another act of self-love.

– Self-care on a physical level is based on four pillars: watching what you eat, exercising, avoiding toxic habits and behaviors and following doctors' orders.

– Don't feel the need to medicate or treat your body when it's not needed. If you're not sick, then your body is fine.

Daily exercise:

BOOST YOUR SELF-CARE

1.   Reflect on how present in your life those four pillars are (watching what you eat, exercising, avoiding toxic habits and behaviors, and following your doctor's orders).

2.   Decide on one improvement for each of them. For example, reducing your meat intake (if it's not contraindicated for your), eating more fruit, seeing a physiotherapist, going to bed earlier, getting a checkup, and so on.

3.   Commit to that improvement. When you've made it, ask yourself to add a new one to your life (remember that we're not talking about weight loss or getting obsessed with the gym, but rather about objectively improving your health). If you look at it as a habit, you'll soon feel much more satisfied and at peace with your body.

Your head is okay

The way you are comes from the genetic and environmental factors that have affected your existence from the moment you were born up until now. Just like with your body, your personality is the result of thousands of genetic combinations and outside factors. There is very little about it that is up to you, so it's no use getting upset over the way you are.

Your personality is predetermined by your genes and you can't change it. Instead of getting frustrated by that, be a sport about it. Your character, on the other hand, is learned and can be modified, and it's equally pointless to get upset over something that you can improve.

So where does the problem lie?

Simply put, you have to accept the things you cannot change and focus on the things you can. For example, an introverted person can't stop being an introvert. They can change their behavior to prevent that personality trait from bringing them problems, but they can't remove it from their DNA because altering their genes is not within their reach.

Introverts have more cortical activity than extroverts, but extroverts are more sensitive to external stimuli. Which is better and which is worse? Who cares?! We can't change one for the other anyway.

Changing your character is possible, but difficult. Firstly, because your primitive brain thinks: "If I've survived so far this way, why risk changing?". Secondly, because you need good stimuli and clear motivators to do it. At the end of the day, why change if you have no guarantee of a reward? And thirdly, change is hard if you don't do it with love and out of love. It's not just me saying that: many personality experts[2] state that love and positive reinforcement are the fuel for personal growth. When you try to change, you should do it, above all, out of self-love.

Stop rejecting your personality and get ready to embrace it. Tell your brain: "We make a great team! Let's train hard so that each of us can do our best work."

Get to know yourself a little better every day

To build real self-love, you need to know yourself. Otherwise, you're living with a stranger and you're not sure whether you like them or not.

---

2 To cite two names: the psychiatrist Carlos Álvarez Vara and the Psychology professor and personality expert Manuel Juan Espinosa.

To know who you are, you don't need to subject yourself to long hours of psychoanalysis: you can begin by looking at your taste in food, sports, music or cities.

I have a personal soft spot for the Proust Questionnaire. It's not a personality test at all – it's an informal interview aimed at getting to know someone's interests and opinions[3].

You might find some of the questions outdated (they are from the late nineteenth century!) and others childish (don't forget that the original was written by a teenage girl), but I like to offer it to my patients as it is. I'll leave it here for you and invite you to take a look at it for yourself:

1. What is your main personality trait?

2. What quality do you like most in a man?

---

3 The Proust Questionnaire was created by Proust's friend Antoinette Faure when they were teenagers. Later, Proust adopted it to use for creating book characters, and it has since been used in interviews, tests, and so on.

3.   What about in a woman?

4.   What do you hope for from your friends?

5.   What's your main flaw?

6.   Your favorite occupation?

7.   Your idea of happiness?

8.   What is your greatest fear?

9.   What do you want to be (when you're older)?

10. What country would you like to live in?

11. Your favorite color?

12. Favorite flower?

13. Favorite bird?

14. Favorite writers?

15. Favorite poets?

16. Favorite fictional hero?

17. Heroine?

18. Favorite music?

19. Painter?

20. Who's your real-life hero?

21. What's your favorite name?

22. What habit do you deplore in other people?

23. What do you hate the most?

24. A character you don't like?

25. A battle you admire?

26. What virtue do you wish you had?

27. How would you like to die?

28. What is your most common state of mind?

29. What flaws do you most indulge in?

30. Do you have a motto?

You might be wondering how a form about favorite flowers and birds can help you to love yourself. Well, this questionnaire is just an example, but I'm sure that some of the questions have made you think and discover something new about yourself. That's what it's about.

There's more to life than the alpha male

I'm sure you've heard of it. The alpha male (the female was added later) is that strong, aggressive, dominant man, without a trace of vulnerability, who imposes *his* law on *his* territory, and everyone is afraid of him. The concept comes from a pretty psychopathic view of the leader of a wolf pack.

The truth is that alpha wolves don't actually force their groups to submit through fear, but rather the opposite: a wolf leader inspires tranquility and sets an example to the rest[4].

---

4 Experts who track the wolves of Yellowstone explain that the leaders are almost never aggressive toward other pack members and that they do things like tend to the weakest cubs and allow themselves to lose when play fighting.

The danger of alpha males in our society comes from the "values" attributed to them: supposedly, these are desirable traits, but they're like something from a teen movie. The alpha male is white, good-looking, middle-class, charismatic, straight, the captain of the high school football team and destined for a high-ranking job where he'll have a lot of money and not a lot of empathy.

What if you're not like that? What if you don't like bossing people around, or your life's goal is not to own a multinational? Are you worth less? Are you too soft? Are you an idiot?

People who defend the idealization of alpha males are people who live in fear. They think that a more diverse and flexible society, where everyone can choose their own destiny and where it's not necessary to rule with an iron fist, will inevitably end in chaos. In reality, what really leads to chaos is teaching people to want to submit to others.

Don't feel obligated to become an alpha male or female, and never think you're a loser if you're not one and have no interest in becoming one.

Summary:

–   You can't change your personality, but you can improve your character and behavior. And that's enough.

–   To love yourself, you need to accept yourself, and to accept yourself you need to know who you are, what drives you, what attracts you and what you avoid.

–   Don't feel obligated to be like others. Change should occur, above all, out of love and respect for yourself.

Daily exercise:

DO YOU REALLY KNOW YOURSELF?

1.   Read and learn about people you admire (it could be your grandpa, Messi or the first woman in space). Discover their tastes, hobbies and daily lives – things outside of their fame.

2.   Compare that information to yourself and find some common areas: you both like dogs, you're both allergic to bananas, you both prefer beach vacations, you both hate crowds, and so on.

3.   This exercise has a dual aim: to get to know yourself better (which we've already said is essential for your self-esteem) and to bring you closer to other people so you can see you're not so different.

Always look for the real "why"

There is a stage in childhood where we keep asking adults around us "why": why are clouds white, why do dogs bark, why do I have to eat my vegetables? When adults reply to the first question, we immediately think of another question about clouds, or dogs, or vegetables, and we ask "why" to the answer we just received.

When we reach adulthood, we stop asking, so that we don't look ignorant or dumb. And worst of all, we stop asking ourselves: we prefer to draw immediate conclusions that give us a sensation of self-sufficiency, rather than ask something and risk admitting we still don't know enough.

Here's what I think: for as long as you draw breath, you should ask questions. Why? Because when you stop questioning things, it's because you've begun to generate your own automatic responses out of fear, arrogance or exhaustion.

And it's okay to be afraid of the unknown or to feel overwhelmed by all the information that exists in the world. But when it comes to ourselves, we should be asking "why" with every new step we take.

Getting to the heart of the matter

Wondering "why" means refusing to be tied down, by yourself or by others. Wondering "why" you do certain things or why you're so sure of something means you won't accept impositions or absolute truths without first making sure they are logical[5].

Let me give you an example of why the barrage of "whys" that children fire when they won't settle for that first answer is so useful.

I often talk to people who say they want to change jobs. My first question is always "why?". Their first answers tend to be complaints about their employers: "My boss is useless", "I've been there for five years without getting promoted", "I'm undervalued there".

I ask them to leave external circumstances aside and answer in the first person, using the verb "want". Then, I hear answers like:

– Because I want to make more money.

– Because I want more responsibility.

---

5 In a few pages, we'll go back to the topic of absolute truths and distorted thought processes.

- Because I want to change sectors.

- Because I want something closer to home.

Even then, these answers don't reveal the real reasons. These are the things people want to change, the "*whats*": more money, a promotion, another company, a new sector. But what we need to find out is why we want those things. Why do we want more money? Why do we want to change sectors?

I try to get to the heart of the matter, where the real reasons for unhappiness lie. That's when people really start to discover their sore points:

- Because it pisses me off that my brother is doing better than me.

- Because I'm embarrassed by my job.

- Because my dad is disappointed in me.

- Because I always dreamed of more.

– Because my partner earns more than me and I'm afraid one day they'll leave me.

We often hide the real "why" out of shame or fear. We cover it up with motives more easily accepted, by ourselves or by society, sometimes subconsciously. But you can't help yourself if you don't dig deep: it's like a doctor only treating the superficial symptoms of an illness without investigating the underlying cause.

You have to get to the bottom of your own "whys", even if the truth is uncomfortable. It's the first step to helping yourself when you're unhappy with something.

Careful with that crystal ball!

I reiterate the "whys" so much because I want to combat the traps that your mind sets: it's time to talk about distorted thinking.

Distorted thinking is a false belief caused by erroneous learning in the past. The problem with these beliefs is not about how we remember the past, but how they condition our present and future, since our actions are more influenced by those beliefs than by reality.

So what does this have to do with loving yourself?

The beliefs you adopt as absolute truths keep you from growing. And, since they're wrong, the longer you hold onto them, the harder it is to accept that mistake since you've continued to make decisions based on it.

How are these thoughts created? Let's look at an example:

Every time I have been to London, it has rained. As such, I believe that in London, it rains every day, and that that's how it will always be. However, I know that's not the case. What's more, even if it really did rain every day, I wouldn't be able to guarantee it would continue that way in the future; I'm not a fortune teller. Even so, I continue to believe that it's always raining in London and always will be.

When do I realize my mistake? When reality stops aligning with what I believe: in other words, when I go to London one day and find that the sun does, in fact, shine there sometimes.

So, what do I do? I have two options: I either accept that I drew a mistaken conclusion, or I try at any cost to hide the truth from myself in order to avoid admitting that I was wrong. Against all logic, we too often go for the second option. Why? Because accepting reality forces us to abandon our beliefs, with all the risk that carries for our system of learning and values that we base our lives on.

The false sense of security of distorted thinking

Distorted thinking is a defense mechanism: its function is to bring security and protection in the face of uncertainty or pain – sometimes even anticipating that pain in order to "keep it under control". What's hiding behind that is fear: fear of failure, of losing control, of not being accepted, and so on.

Distorted thinking is the highest level of the so-called "comfort zone".

Before continuing, I want to clarify that experiencing distorted thinking does not in any way make you crazy. In fact, many of these thoughts are the fruit of the education you have received and most of us have experienced them at some point in our lives, maybe without even realizing it.

Let's look at the main mechanisms by which these thoughts are created:

1. **Filtering or exaggeration:** Distorted thinking arises from exaggeration of the negatives of an occurrence and a minimization of the positives.

2. **Polarized thinking:** The facts are judged in black and white, with no space for any middle ground.

3. **Over-generalization:** A general conclusion is drawn from a single fact.

4. **Reading others' minds:** We think we know what others are thinking by interpreting some of their actions.

5. **Catastrophic vision:** We expect the worst of a situation even though there are far likelier possibilities.

6. **Personalization:** We think that our environments are reacting to us.

7. **Culpability:** We tend to systematically blame others for our own suffering, or on the flip side, we shoulder all of the blame for it.

8. **Duty:** In order for the world to work, everyone should behave the way they "know" how. Since they don't, the world is how it is.

9. **Emotional reasoning:** What we feel in a given moment becomes fact.

10. **Control and justice fallacies:** We act in a certain way because we believe it is the way to get something (even if it doesn't really depend on our actions).

11. **Being right:** Life becomes an endless battle to prove that we are always right.

12. **Divine or future reward:** We inflict suffering on ourselves because we believe we will get recognition for it in the future.

13. **Labeling:** We define people by something they did one time or because of prejudice.

All of these are forms of reasoning conditioned by fear. This is why you need to identify and combat these thoughts, comparing them to reality as often as necessary.

Summary:

–   Always questioning why you do the things you do keeps you free from being held back by yourself or by others.

–   Regularly comparing your beliefs to reality is the best way of not accepting impositions or absolute truths. Don't take anything for granted.

–   Distorted thinking is the highest level of the so-called "comfort zone".

–   False beliefs bring you a short-term sense of security, but in the long term they limit your freedom to act.

Daily exercise:

<u>WHY DO YOU DO THAT?</u>

1. Think about something you do regularly and which carries some weight in your life, whether because of the amount of time you dedicate to it or because of how long you've been doing it for. It can be something you like doing or something you do out of obligation: working in an office, going for Sunday dinners at your parents' house, paying taxes, watching your daughter play basketball, or whatever else.

2. Subject that activity to a barrage of "whys" until you reach the ultimate reason. Assess whether that ultimate reason makes sense to you, if you identify with it or if, on the other hand, it's something you imposed on yourself but which you could do without.

3. The aim is to be aware of what your actions are responding to and to what extent they

align with your goals. The more aware of this you are, the better your self-esteem will be.

DAY 9

Embrace your anxiety

We're going to dedicate today's session to public enemy number one: anxiety. The aim is for you to stop seeing it as a paralyzing poison and start loving it.

Loving it?! But it makes my life a nightmare!

No, your anxiety does not make your life a nightmare: it's just the messenger. What makes your life a nightmare is what altered your nervous system and put it on permanent high alert.

Anxiety is a defense mechanism that tells you something's not right. The problem is that we're not always able to interpret that warning, instead getting frustrated and stressed by the symptoms it causes.

To avoid this, many therapists train their patients to ignore the symptoms of anxiety, when what we should be doing is listening to it.

Anxiety that gets ignored becomes something else: physical pain, panic attacks, phobias, depression, and so on.

To overcome it, you need to work along two lines: first, to find its origin, and second, to reach a day-to-day agreement with anxiety.

What is that origin?

In a way, anxiety is your brain screaming: "Danger! We're facing a real threat! Run!"

Your brain perceives an imminent threat to your physical or emotional integrity and activates your alarm system, which is the sympathetic part of your autonomous nervous system: your heart rate and breathing get faster, your pupils dilate, your mouth gets dry... These are natural physiological reactions to "danger", and they are how your body prepares to "get you to safety". It's what would happen if, for example, you found yourself face to face with a hungry-looking tiger.

However, usually, that "tiger" is camouflaged and you need to work introspectively in order to find it.

That camouflaged tiger might be:

- A deep-seated fear.

- A prolonged period of stress that you had so far been able to tolerate.

- A life crisis.

- A significant loss.

- A trauma you thought you had overcome.

- ...

For example: if you have held a belief for your entire life that brought you a sense of security and then one day you discovered that it was wrong, it's likely you would feel anxiety. Until you accept the "new situation", your brain will remain on high alert.

I once helped Emma, a twenty-four-year-old patient who had begun suffering very intense panic attacks for no apparent reason. When we began working together, we saw that Emma was in a very good place in her life: she had the job of her dreams as a doctor, she was in a great relationship, she was healthy, she had friends, projects... Where was the tiger?

To her surprise, the tiger was associated with her mother, who she said she was very close to. When we looked in depth at her relationship with her mother, Emma begin to display a lot of shame: she felt indebted to her and thought it was wrong to criticize her "after all the sacrifices she's made for me". We soon realized that her mother had used manipulation and emotional blackmail to control Emma "for her own good", and that at some point during her childhood, Emma had begun to deny herself in order to please her mother. Now, she felt cheated, but she couldn't confront her mother about it because it was thanks to her that she had "become someone".

That contradiction had led Emma to an emotional imbalance that had eventually blown up in her face. She had to get her emotions in order and reinterpret her past in order to move on with her life.

Anxiety simply tells us that we have unfinished business. If you want to eliminate anxiety, you need to face that task and finish it by working on acceptance and making changes to your thinking in relation to the problem.

And during that process of introspection when facing your tiger... you will have to deal with anxiety in your everyday life. Let's look at how to do that.

How to deal with anxiety

If you suffer from or have suffered from anxiety, you'll know that it can manifest through many different emotions and physical reactions, from nausea and a racing heart to catastrophic thoughts. That's why everyone needs to find their own methods for dealing with it[6].

A few strategies include:

1. **Talk to it openly:** Talk to your anxiety when you feel it. Ask it why it has come to you. Listen to it, feel everything it evokes and accept it as part of the message that you need to decipher.

---

6 Remember that anxiety will keep coming back until you can discover and accept the original reason for it.

2. **Then, politely ask it to leave:** "Thanks for coming and bringing me this message, but you need to leave now", "I understand why you're here, but I've got it under control, you can go, I'm in charge now."

3. **Give it an appointment**: Set some time aside in the day to dedicate to your anxiety. Your nervous system will calm down if it knows there is some time set aside for its messages. What you're telling your brain is: "Since I can't talk to you right now, I'll devote some time later to properly listen to what you have to tell me."

4. **Use distracting activities**: Surges of anxiety tend to disappear after a few minutes. However, for those few minutes, they really take over. To make that difficult time pass as fast as possible, focus on an activity that demands your attention. Listen carefully to a song, cook something to a recipe, call someone on the phone, meditate, write a letter, and so on. Anything that quickly

distracts you until the surge of anxiety has faded away.

5. **Show it that you can do it:** Anxiety is your own insecurity telling you that you can't do something. Don't get mad at it; remember that it's just your brain's way of protecting you from pain or failure. To calm it down, find ways to prove that it can "trust" you. Small achievements, little victories that add up and bring you confidence. For example: if your anxiety goes sky-high when you have to speak in public, start by explaining something mundane to one of your neighbors. Then, increase your audience to three or four people in different situations and observe how it gets easier each time. If you're terrified of swimming in the sea, get yourself a summer calendar and commit to going half a step further into the water each day.

6. **Show it some test results:** Anxiety often comes dressed up as a heart attack or a very convincing mental health episode. To make

yourself feel better, ask your doctor for tests to show you're not having any kind of attack or serious medical episode.

Summary:

–   Anxiety is just the messenger.

–   Anxiety is your brain activating its alarm system. Instead of getting scared, listen to it and understand why it's going off.

–   To overcome anxiety, you need a two-pronged approach: one, to reach everyday agreements with it and two, to find its origin so you can switch it off.

–   Remember that anxiety on its own is harmless: it can't give you a heart attack or make you schizophrenic or cause you to lose control. Those are just the disguises it wears to get your attention.

Daily exercise:

<u>YOUR ANXIETY JOURNAL</u>

1. Get a journal (it can be a simple notebook), and turn it int your Anxiety Journal: note down the days you feel anxiety, what the situation was, what you were doing, when it went away, and so on.

2. Keep a record of your anxiety for a while and examine it regularly for patterns and coincidences. That will help you to apply strategies at critical points, anticipate possible surges of anxiety and prove to yourself that it always fades away.

3. The aim is to lose your fear of anxiety and live with it for as long as you can't eliminate it. In time, the journal will also help to strengthen your self-esteem, as you will begin to see progress in your own management of your anxiety.

DAY 10

All your emotions are valid

While accepting your body is enough of a challenge, accepting the emotions you're ashamed of is an even bigger one.

The first thing you need to understand is that emotions are information. In the same way you feel cold, thirsty or itchy, you can feel afraid, calm, humiliated, betrayed, flattered or cheerful. It's simply information that your brain sends the ship's captain, which is you.

Emotions are tied to the human condition itself and it is not possible not to feel them. So why do we reject and judge them?

It's probably because we've been driven to do so in order to prevent them from getting "out of control" and knocking us off balance. But in reality, we will get knocked sometimes – that's just life! When we fall in love, when a loved one passes away, when we lose our job or when someone lets us down, that balance gets disturbed. Every new stage, every new experience, every fall and every goal achieved makes us feel things, and it's pointless to deny that.

So it's okay to be overcome by emotion. It's okay to feel pity, affection, sorrow, disgust or terror. It's okay to feel totally defeated every now and again. And it's okay to want to jump for joy.

If your own emotions confuse you or make you feel uneasy, ask yourself: "Why do I think that feeling this way is bad or shameful?", "How am I supposed to feel?", "How would I like to feel instead?".

Educating your emotions doesn't mean burying them: it means learning from them so you can act accordingly.

Your emotions are for those who value them

I'm a firm believer in not hiding your emotions. However, they don't always come at the best time and not everyone is perfect for sharing them with. Your emotions are not for everyone.

Imagine you made some amazing chocolate chip cookies. To cool them, you leave them on the windowsill (fifties-style). And since your window is at street level, the aroma attracts passers-by. Some people come up to your window. What's their intention? Well, some will want to compare your cookies with the ones they make at home. Others will be looking for a way to steal them. Others will want to know who made these little delights and maybe chat to you a while and share baking tips. Other people will fall in love with your cookies and offer to swap them for some pastries they made. You catch my drift.

Well, those cookies are your emotions. And, like cookies, emotions draw people in. It's instinctive and we can't avoid it. But, as you can see, not everyone has the same intentions when they approach your cookies.

We can all remember a time when getting swept up by emotion hurt us. So isn't it safer to keep them locked away?

In truth, no. Firstly, because that's impossible to do, and secondly because it dehumanizes you.

The wonderful people who love you, the people who value you, hope to share your more emotional side with you. In fact, you can't truly love someone if they can't access your emotions.

You are not "too emotional"

I often hear male patients of mine complaining that their wives and girlfriends are unstable, too intense or too hard to understand emotionally. Similarly, I hear many women ashamed of "feeling too much" or of being "emotional rollercoasters", in their own words.

Lots of disagreements between men and women relating to emotions come from the differences between our limbic systems[7]. Add to that the effects of sex hormones at many life stages of women that don't correspond to those of men: menstrual cycles, pregnancy, post-partum, to give the best-known examples, lead to changes that are natural (I mean, normal from a physiological point of view) and that translate

---

[7] I'm not reducing reality to men versus women, just explaining what I have seen in my career when dealing with problems in heterosexual relationships.

into "mood swings" women are the first to fall prey to.

You can add cultural factors into this mix here: we live in a patriarchal world where women tend to bear the brunt. While men can focus on professional success, women are expected to meet high expectations in many different areas.

Finally, several studies state that on average, women tend to be more empathetic than men. This means that they are more sensitive to others' emotions.

Because of all of this, even in contexts of full equality, men and women feel things differently. And whenever the way that men feel is considered "right" and the way women feel "wrong", suffering and conflict are guaranteed to occur.

Here is an example of the differences between the acceptance of emotions in traditionally masculine and feminine areas: many countries normalize male emotions in relation to sports. It's rare for a man to be ashamed of "feeling too much" on the day of a cup final. On the other hand, a woman crying over a terrible event thousands of miles away is seen as weak or immature: "that's just how the world works" or "but that happens every day".

Men and women feel things differently. Invalidating, ignoring or judging the emotions of the other gender is not just unfair, it's totally pointless. Instead, let's make an effort to empathize more with the way the people around us feel.

Summary:

– If your own emotions make you feel confused or uneasy, ask yourself: "Why do I think that feeling this way is wrong or shameful?"

– Emotions are information. In the same way that we feel cold, thirsty or itchy, we can feel scared, calm, humiliated, happy, betrayed or flattered. It's part of human nature and there is no use ignoring it.

– Men and women feel things differently. Invalidating, ignoring or judging the emotions of the other gender is not just unfair, it's totally pointless.

– It's impossible to truly love someone (yourself included) if they can't access your emotions or if they reject them.

Daily exercise:

YOUR EMOTIONS ARE NORMAL

1.   Make a list of all the emotions you can think of: sadness, happiness, fear, uncertainty, disgust, surprise, scorn, love, calm, insecurity, and so on.

2.   For six months, mark the date with each emotion as you feel it. If you can, add a brief reflection on why you think that feeling arose, how it made you feel to feel it (weak, ridiculous, calm, ashamed...) and what needed to happen to stop you feeling that way.

3.   In time, you will see the emotions you feel most often and begin to understand how they work and what they are telling you, as well as gradually being able to more easily accept your own emotions.

The three horsemen of Evil: envy, jealousy and guilt

Accepting your emotions doesn't mean that you have to be a prisoner to them, much less that they should be the ones to determine your actions.

Some emotions considered negative, such as envy, jealousy and guilt, are not dangerous in and of themselves (we have already talked about how emotions are neither good nor bad on their own), but they become a hazard when they force you to act or think in certain ways. For example: my envy of my neighbor's new car is not dangerous in itself, but if I don't know how to control that emotion and it leads me to commit an act of vandalism like slashing his tires, then it has become dangerous.

It's one thing to accept that you will feel envious at certain times and another to believe that acting on that envy will benefit you in some way.

How to help your envy

Envy is the frustration of not having something you want and that other people do. We tend to suffer it in silence because it damages our image and makes us feel vulnerable: behind it, there are self-esteem issues and a childlike sense of fairness. Fairness? Yes, because we think: "It's not fair that our neighbor, who's not smart at all, makes more money than we do!".

The big problem with envy (outside of making us feel bad) is that it makes our satisfaction depend on things that happen to other people: we feel frustrated when the neighbor is doing well and get a burst of dopamine when something bad happens to him. That means that we're relinquishing control over our own wellbeing! Doesn't that seem kind of absurd and risky to you?

Fortunately, envy can be tamed. It may never disappear completely, but you can make it less toxic. How?

First, interrogate it. What is bugging you so much? Is it the lack of the object itself, or is it feeling that someone has it who doesn't deserve it as much as you do? Why don't they deserve it? And why, if you deserve it more, don't you have it? Who is that down to?

Then, we come to the sixty-four-million-dollar question: is there something you can do to obtain that thing you envy? If so, then get to work. If not, treat the frustration as a loss, mourn it a little.

If you're envious of your brother's relationship with his partner, instead of sabotaging it or unloading your frustration onto your own partner, look at what you can do to improve your own relationship. If you're envious of someone else's money, maybe it's time to rethink your job or, even better, your concept of happiness.

When you start working on it, the envy disappears instantly. It's like magic, but it's not.

Envy is a call to action: not to others, but to yourself.

Jealousy, a pointless prison

Although they are often confused with each other, jealousy and envy are not the same thing. While envy is the desire for something you don't have, jealousy is the fear of losing something you do have: someone's love. Children feel jealous when their mothers are affectionate with their other children, dogs when they see their owner petting another animal, and most people when they see that their partner has attracted someone else's interest. Jealousy is the fear that the other person will discover there is *someone better* to give their love to and will take it away from you.

Jealousy speaks to our concept of love and our emotional dependency. The antidote is firstly to understand that you can't force anyone to choose you (love has to be offered freely and voluntarily) and secondly to work on your dependence. This means asking yourself what would happen if you did lose that person's love. How would you feel? What does that say about you? If it would really end you, doesn't that mean you've put your happiness in someone else's hands? Or is the jealousy because you feel inferior and are afraid that people will figure you out?

Your partner has the right to leave you for someone else. That's a fact. It might hurt to hear it, but no one is anyone's property. You're free to leave them, too.

I'm not defending a lack of commitment, cheating or selfishness. I'm saying that jealousy is pointless, because if someone is with you it's because they've chosen you. For as long as they're with you, jealousy makes no sense, and it's a lack of respect for the relationship and your trust in that person. And if that person decides to cheat or leave, it's not worth getting jealous over, because that won't change anything.

That's why, no matter what's going on around us, jealousy is a prison we build around ourselves.

Feelings of guilt

Let me make one thing clear: no one can love themselves while consumed by guilt.

Guilt is the discomfort we feel when we know that, at some point, we did the wrong thing when we could have done the right thing. It's a kind of moral self-reproach.

But guilt is also a powerful weapon of manipulation. In an environment where the limits of personal responsibility are blurred and an individual's self-esteem is affected, it's easy to make them feel guilty to get something out of them in return for "redemption". This turns guilt into a one-way ticket to emotional blackmail.

Whether the guilt is being shouldered alone or whether it allows someone else to exploit it for personal gain, it is counterproductive for personal growth and you won't make progress until you get away from it.

How can you do that?

Let's look at the first situation: how to overcome feelings of guilt over something you did wrong. This is a five-step process:

1. **Fully admit it.** Yes, you were wrong, you hurt others and you feel badly about it. And yes, it was a shameful mistake, although at

that point it offered you some kind of benefit which you now regret.

2. **Try to understand why you behaved in that way.** Don't look for an excuse to keep the moral high ground, but seek to understand what you were hoping to achieve through that action with a view to never making the same mistake again.

3. **Ask the people you hurt for forgiveness, sincerely and with no buts.** It's worthless to say: "I'm sorry, I'm just like that" or "Forgive me, but this wouldn't have happened if you hadn't...".

4. **Take every possible action to try and repair the damage you caused.** If it was about money, give it back, if you betrayed someone's trust, try to rebuild it with time and sacrifice, if you stepped on someone's toes to get the glory, renounce it and go public.

5. **Commit to never doing it again, and keep your promise.** Being forgiven doesn't give you carte blanche to do it again.

It is possible that, even after all that, you will still feel badly or the other person won't forgive you (they don't have to). But you will have done everything in your power to make up for it and to be better, and that will alleviate your guilt in time.

So what happens when someone makes you feel guilty unfairly or for their own benefit?

What happens then is that you shoulder that guilt without realizing you didn't do anything wrong, or that someone is using it to exploit you.

Here, it's important to know where the limits of your responsibility lie. The things you have been taught play a key role in this – not just things you were told at home, but also at school and by culture. If you were taught guilt, it's likely that you will be a perpetually guilty-feeling adult.

Many experts, from Nathaniel Branden to Luis Rojas Marcos[8], highlight that education by the Church is a powerful generator of guilt. I agree: when a religion preaches total self-sacrifice and tells you that you are guilty simply of existing (you're a child of original sin!), that religion is attacking your most fundamental human rights.

The same occurs when someone takes advantage of your failings (either real or perceived) to hurt you: it could be your partner, relatives, boss, and so on. No one has the right to foster or exploit your feelings of guilt for their own gain.

---

[8] 8 A psychologist and a psychiatrist who have produced important work in the fields of self-esteem and happiness, respectively.

Summary:

–   Accepting your emotions doesn't mean you have to be a slave to them, much less that they should determine your actions for you.

–   Envy is a call to action, but positive action.

–   Jealousy is a prison we build around ourselves external to what is happening around us.

–   Feelings of guilt are personal and non-transferable. Learning from bad behavior and repairing the damage done is the path to relieving it.

–   No one has the right to exploit your guilt for their own gain.

Daily exercise:

I'M SO ENVIOUS!

1. Today, we're going to switch roles: you'll be my therapist and I'll be your patient. As a patient, my problem is that I am horribly, intensely envious of rich people.

2. With the information in this book and your own resources, would you be able to design a strategy to help me? What would you say to me? What thoughts do you think I should change?

3. On the one hand, the aim of this exercise is to naturalize emotions considered shameful or weak, and on the other, it's to encourage you to create your own strategies for emotional self-care.

Your journey so far is valid

We all have a past. And in every past, there are dark, sad or cruel times. In fact, in my experience, I would say most of us are carrying guilt or shame around certain moments in our lives. But that shouldn't stop us from loving and accepting ourselves unconditionally, starting now.

You know why?

Because the past is a place to learn from, not a place to live.

And you know why else?

Because, as a therapist, I think it would be fine to spend all your time thinking about your past if not for the fact you have something much more important to think about: your present and future!

Your past is an archive, and it's always there for you to consult. But you don't have to carry it with you every moment of every day: it's not going anywhere and no one can steal it from you.

Whether it's happy or painful, your past is fine the way it is. I'm not saying the trauma or injustice you may have suffered is any less important, nor are any of the joyful moments you've experienced – what I'm saying is that the past is not moving. It's you who needs to be moving. If your past makes you suffer in the present, you need to find a new way to relate to your memories.

You can be happy and love yourself even with a sad past. Even if you have not yet overcome the after-effects of life's hard knocks. You don't have to wait to be "clean" to embrace your life. Every morning when you wake up, you are clean.

Allow yourself not to be able to get over something right now. You might get over it in the future, but for today, validate yourself and don't punish yourself.

You are not your mistakes

Whoa! It turns out that, when I look back on my life... it's full of mistakes! How could I fail at this, or that? How could I act in that way? How stupid, what an idiot I was!

I could spend all day thinking that. And what I've learned, from my own experience and that of others, is that what we are most ashamed of is not the big mistakes in our lives (we tend to contextualize those quite compassionately), but the endless slip-ups, the carelessness, silliness, confusion, naivete or arrogance, pathetic acts and statements out of turn that are etched onto our memories.

Our lives are plagued with mistakes, but also with good decisions. Why do we identify more closely with the former?

As people, we hate making mistakes because we believe that they define us. However, successful people know that mistakes are simply the fruit of their actions.

It's estimated that most of us will take three good decisions to emotionally compensate for an equivalent bad one. That's exhausting!

So, what should you do? You should look at it with the same mindset as a scientist working on a vaccine: test, check the result, if it's not valid, try something else, and keep trying until you find the correct option.

Let go

If you were a hot air balloon, I would tell you: "Let go of the rope and you'll fly!".

You're not a balloon, but the advice still stands: let go, say goodbye, close the loop. Don't wait for "the right moment" to leave something behind. Let something end badly. In fact, some things will get broken along the way and you will have to abandon them without closure: a relationship, an unfinished project, an adventure you never went on, a last time, a promise you couldn't keep... It's a shame, and I wish it weren't so, but it will sometimes be inevitable.

Focus on the adventures, projects and relationships to come, and on your desire for things to go right this time. That's the only thing you can do about the rope that's keeping you from flying.

To sum up, let me leave you with this quote from Carl Bard: "Though no one can go back and make a brand new start, anyone can start from now and make a brand new ending."

Summary:

- Your past is something you have, not something you are.

- The past is a place you learn from, not a place you live in.

- Mistakes are a fact of life, but they don't define you. They are the fruit of some of our actions: you are not the mistake itself.

- Our lives are full of mistakes, but also of good decisions. Don't identify more with the former than with the latter.

Daily exercise:

TRANSFER YOUR PAST TO SOMEONE ELSE

1. Identify an event in your past that you find hard to accept. It doesn't necessarily need to be traumatic – it can be a simple embarrassing moment.

2. Now, imagine that it wasn't you who experienced that event, but someone you love: your mother, partner, son... And imagine that the emotions you feel are being felt by that person. Do you think their suffering is justified? How would you help them to feel better?

3. If you get into the habit of analyzing events from your past as if they had happened to someone you care about, you'll soon relativize your own guilt or shame around them and begin to judge your past more compassionately.

DAY 13

A little respect!

We're going to dedicate the middle days of our bootcamp to the most important concept associated with self-esteem: self-respect.

Unlike self-esteem (everyone knows what it is, everyone talks about it), self-respect is still a great unknown in the field of personal growth. But it's absolutely essential.

From when we're little, we're taught to respect others. Our parents and teachers tell us off if we behave badly with other children or don't share our toys, and that's great, but sometimes they miss out the fundamental part where we know our own rights, too.

When we're taught to be obedient, to please others, to do things without taking our own feelings into account, to endure injustice or to believe that we are inadequate, we learn to invalidate ourselves and reject our own needs. As a result, we end up lacking in respect for ourselves or allowing others to do so. Our inner caregiver betrays us.

Self-respect is knowing that you have a series of inalienable rights that do not depend on your success, obedience or usefulness to others. Practicing self-respect means not renouncing those rights, regardless of anyone else.

Even if you're aware of it, you may not always know how to change things in order to command respect. Over the next few pages, we will look at how to respect yourself and how to demand that others respect you, too.

Believe me: so many things will change when you finally learn to say, "I don't deserve this".

Your emotional rights

Everyone is born equal and with the same right to strive for not just survival but for wellbeing.

To achieve this, it's essential that you can express yourself and defend your needs, wants and opinions without repercussions. That is known as assertiveness, and it gives rise to a "card" of emotional rights:

1.   The right to be treated with respect and dignity.

2.   The right to hold and express our own feelings and opinions.

3.   The right to be listened to and taken seriously.

4.   The right to judge our own needs, establish priorities and make decisions.

5.   The right to say "no" without guilt.

6. The right to ask for what we want, understanding that the other person also has the right to say no.

7. The right to change.

8. The right to make mistakes.

9. The right to ask for information and to be informed.

10. The right to get what we paid for (an item, service, coverage, and so on).

11. The right to decide not to be assertive (without stepping on others' rights).

12. The right to be independent.

13. The right to decide what to do with our own time, body, property, and so on.

14. The right to be successful.

15. The right to enjoy ourselves.

16. The right to rest and solitude.

17. The right to better ourselves or even be better than others.

You might be thinking: "But these rights get violated all the time!". You're right, they do. But just because they get violated doesn't mean they don't exist. Whatever the situation, never believe that you don't have those rights.

Knowing this list of rights is, above all, about you, and it functions as a thermostat for the environment you're in.

Summary:

– All people are born equal and with the same right to seek our own survival but also wellbeing.

– When we're taught to be obedient, to please others, to endure mistreatment or to believe that we're inadequate, we learn to reject ourselves as complete people.

– We all have a list of emotional rights we should be aware of.

Daily exercise:

YOUR RED LINES

1. Based on what I've said about emotional rights and using your own resources, think about some situations where your rights might be compromised. For example: an inappropriate request (for intimacy, for excessive trust, for illicit or illegal activity, for professional mistreatment, etc.).

2. Decide how you would say no to that request in a diplomatic way but without betraying yourself.

3. Get used to doing this exercise regularly, even if mentally or with made-up situations: little by little, self-respect will begin to come more naturally to you, until you know how to defend your emotional rights without even realizing you're doing it.

Defend your boundaries

Now that you understand self-respect on a theoretical level, you need to put it into practice. It's time to defend your personal boundaries, and there are four steps to doing that:

1. Inform.

2. Ask.

3. Insist.

4. Distance yourself.

First, a warning: boundaries are not set for other people, they are set for yourself. Their goal is not to make others change (if they do, even better!) but to mark out where you yourself will change – in other words, when you will say "enough". Boundaries are for you.

Let's imagine that someone close to you is treating you badly. They've been doing it for a while, so others assume it doesn't bother you. No one expects you to demand change at this point.

But one day, you politely tell that person that it does bother you **(Step 1)**. You don't have to ask them to or give endless explanations about why it annoys you. Nor do you have to tell them what you intend to do if they don't stop. Step 1 is simply to inform.

That person will either stop... or they won't. If they don't, move on to Step 2.

Step 2: Ask that person to do what they should have already done: stop their behavior. This time, do it in writing or in a voice message (email, WhatsApp, etc.). The person will go on the defensive: "But why? What's so bad about it?". You don't have to answer anything; this isn't a debate.

That person finally stops... even if just for a while. Or they change tack, but keep on violating your boundaries. It's time to go to Step 3.

Step 3: Insist. Insisting aims to tell the other person that you're not going to stop and that both of you will lose out if they don't change (in truth, you won't lose anything, but the other person doesn't know that). This time, try to get proof of their responses and their behaviors (easy with cellphones). He or she should feel that you're prepared to give up your job, family or relationship if this carries on. Don't argue, don't over-explain yourself, just remind them that you already asked them politely to change and they didn't do it. Don't be afraid of causing a scene, even if you find it awkward.

If their reactions go: "You're crazy!", "This bothers you too?", "Are you trying to tell me what to do?", and continues to disrespect you, go to the last step.

Step 4: Distance yourself. Cut ties. If it's a member of your family, stop seeing them and everyone who openly takes their side (you don't need to try to make people comfortable if you feel violated). If it's a work colleague, tell a superior about the situation and let them know you intend to leave your job right away. Resign. Get up from your desk. Get your things and go. Distance yourself.

Don't listen to proposals of "mediation" or "making peace". The time for mediation has passed; that was Step 1.

In any place or situation, if peace comes at the price of compromising your dignity or freedom, that place does not deserve peace and does not deserve you.

Summary:

–   Personal boundaries should always be respected, even though this sometimes doesn't happen.

–   Personal boundaries are for yourself, to show you where you need to say "enough".

–   In any place or situation, if peace comes the price of compromising your dignity or freedom, that place does not deserve peace and does not deserve you

–   The four steps to defending your boundaries when someone is disrespecting them are, in this order: 1) Inform the person you feel disrespected, 2) Ask for a change in attitude to repair the situation, 3) Insist on it once more, and 4) Distance yourself.

Daily exercise:

THE ABUSIVE NEIGHBOR

1.   Imagine a new neighbor has moved into your building with three dogs who bark constantly and make a mess, and the person is not respecting others in the building.

2.   Based on the four steps to defending your boundaries that I have explained in this chapter, design a plan for taking that neighbor on. Remember not to give in to any reasoning from the abusive neighbor, no matter how logical it may seem.

3.   When you practice this exercise in your daily life, you'll become better at foreseeing conflict and abusive responses and you will be better prepared to tackle them.

Protect your time, protect your space

In the same way that you have to delimit the hours you spend working or running errands, you should guard your free time so you can invest it in whatever you want.

If you're like most people, you have a few hours a week to spend on leisure. People normally socialize during those hours, and that's fine, since good times are better with company. But, once more, you need to put yourself first.

Below, I'm going to give you my **Ten Commandments** for free time. Of course, you can change or add to it as you see fit:

1. Thou shalt not waste time arguing with strangers or people you will not see again.

2. Thou shalt not go out if you do not want to.

3. Thou shalt not stay out late if you only wanted a quick drink and to go home.

4. Thou shalt not agree to spend your free time with people who do not interest you.

5. Thou shalt not participate in parties or traditions contrary to your values.

6. Thou shalt not feel obligated to always reply to people on social media, nor to have an opinion on everything.

7. Thou shalt not become closer to people than you want to.

8.   Thou shalt not allow people to know you if you do not want them to know you.

9.   Thou shalt not renounce activities you enjoy.

10. Thou shalt not accept that all your free time belongs to your partner/family/political party/friendship group.

Protect your home, protect your stuff

Your home is your refuge. Spend time getting it the way you want; there are endless ways to make your home a part of you. If you share it with someone, negotiate so that you both feel happy with the place where you live.

Your home should be the place where you and your people feel most at ease. It doesn't have to be magazine cover worthy (but if it is and that works for you, then great!).

Instead of having a home that "pleases" other people, just try to keep it clean, tidy and maintained for you. Why? Because that does more for your self-respect than the approval of armchair decorators. In addition, a tidy and orderly house will save you a lot of time, it's easier to maintain economically and it favors rest, fun and concentration.

On the other hand, self-respect is also expressed through your own habits and way of doing things at home, from the way you celebrate Christmas or decorate for Halloween to the declaration that Wednesday is pizza day. Like the famous Spanish marketing slogan: "Welcome to the Independent Republic of Your Home".

I don't mean that I'm inflexible in my "kingdom": if I invite someone for dinner and I know they don't eat meat, I won't cook meat because I want them to feel at ease as my guest. I think you understand what I'm saying.

Summary:

–   Your free time is your own. Sharing it involves negotiation, but that doesn't mean always betraying yourself.

–   Don't just accept that all your free time belongs to your partner/family/political party/friendship group.

–   Your home is another way to care for and love yourself. Treat it with respect.

Daily exercise:

WHO DO YOU TALK TO?

1. Review the Ten Commandments of free time and select the point or points where you most fall down. For example: "I get sucked into arguments with strangers on social media" (first commandment).

2. Seek out a situation where you normally dive in and argue (a controversial news item, an unfair sports result, etc.). Be aware of that situation.

3. Make a conscious decision not to comment, no matter how badly you want to. How do you feel at that moment? What about at the end of that day? Was it really that important to participate in the argument? Note all of that down for future reference, when you're tempted to fall into that trap again.

Don't be a people pleaser

Fitting in socially is so complicated that we often invent strategies to be accepted by a given social group, beginning with our families and ending with our most superficial relationships. We become "people pleasers".

Unfortunately, many adults learned to be people pleasers during their childhoods: unstable or abusive parents lead little ones to feel obligated to please their loved ones, even at the cost of their own dignity and true selves.

A people pleaser is, in essence, a scared person. They live in fear of being left out or that someone will discover who they *really are inside*.

The truth is that neither of those things (being left out of a group or showing your true self) are as harmful as living to please other people.

Of course, we all like to please people at times. In fact, it is necessary, not just for getting along but also for personal growth. But it should be an act of free will, not the result of blackmail.

So when is pleasing others an act of free will and when is it the result of blackmail?

The difference is the taste it leaves in your mouth: even if the act itself is the same (an innocent favor a relative asks of you, for example), when the emotions it leaves you with are positive – you feel at peace, proud and content – it's an act of free will. If the emotions are murkier – relief mixed with insecurity or the sensation you've betrayed yourself – then be very careful about what you're doing.

How to stop being a people pleaser

The first thing to do is observe yourself and begin to make small changes. For example: don't fake your tastes and preferences regarding leisure and free time. Don't say that you love a restaurant or series if you think it's awful. Stop taking part in activities you don't feel like doing if you find you never get the chance to do activities you do like. Then, try putting a plan or change into action and watch the reactions of those around you. If your suggestions are always ignored, don't get mad: just get ready to leave.

Don't do anything that makes you uncomfortable just because "we always do this" or because "they'll be mad if I don't".

If they only love you when you act a certain way, they really don't love you at all.

Family is not everything

Lots of people are lucky enough to grow up with healthy, functional family backgrounds. And when I say "functional", I mean *it works*: whether it's a nuclear or a single-parent family, rich or just getting by, with healthy members or living with illness, functional means it adapts to the circumstances to guarantee the wellbeing and correct development of all its members equally.

Sadly, others are not so lucky.

When "family" is a synonym for abusive behavior, pejorative treatment, neglect, coercion, violence or love with conditions on it, family is not everything. What's more, you don't owe a family like that anything.

Even if your family paid for your studies or threw you nice birthday parties when you were little, if the price you paid for that was unfairly high, that family does not deserve your loyalty.

You don't owe anything to a loving and functional family, either: the love you give should be voluntary, not repayment of a debt.

I want to clarify that I love my parents and will always take care of them, because I want to. I'm not encouraging doing the opposite. But I would never tell a patient they were obligated to love their parents if they felt they had been treated unfairly or disrespectfully by them.

Don't declare war on your family if that will make you feel worse. Distance yourself silently, and if you can't do it physically, space out gatherings and distance yourself emotionally. Don't continue to subject yourself to what's expected of you or to "how it's always been in this family".

Having children is not an investment in one's future, nor is it a business to live off and profit from, materially or emotionally. Children are not their parents' property.

Summary:

– Don't stay in a place where you're uncomfortable just because "it's always been that way".

– If someone only loves you in a certain way, they actually don't love you at all.

– Love with abusive conditions, love by halves or intermittent love do not deserve your unconditional love in return; they deserve your distance.

– There is life beyond your original family. Your real family will be the one you decide to create with members who love and respect each other, whether or not they share a last name.

– Children are not their parents' property.

Daily exercise:

I DO IT BECAUSE I WANT TO

1.   Think about a situation in the past where you did something for someone else. It doesn't have to be a big thing: it could be going to pick your friend up from the airport, helping out a neighbor, hosting a barbecue for your extended family.

2.   Remember all the emotions you felt surrounding the event, both when you did it (hope, pride in yourself, anger, rage, annoyance, etc.) and when you received others' feedback (you felt good, cheated, underappreciated, valued, etc.).

3.   Based on the above, decide now whether you should have done what you did and whether you would do it again. With practice, you'll be able to make grand gestures for others without feeling obligated to please them for its own sake.

What would you do if you had no fear?

I tend to ask my patients this question when they're not sure what their path should be or they don't dare to change a situation that's harming them.

Their first responses to the question "What would you do if you had no fear?" are usually at opposite ends of a spectrum: they're either very restrained ("I guess I would let some time go by and then ask for that raise again") or totally extreme ("I'd hire a hitman to beat my boss up"). I encourage people to say crazy stuff because it reveals their true desires and needs that had been repressed for so long in order to be "correct".

Then, the answers bring a spark to people's eyes: "If I had no fear, I would resign and create my own firm", "If I had no fear, I would tell my partner I want to go back to live in my hometown", "If I had no fear, I would ask that person out".

I remember the case of Alberto, a lawyer who wanted a career change but didn't dare tell his partner because it would mean bringing in less money. The thing was that Alberto had been working for many years at a firm where he was unhappy. He dreamed of setting up his own company for young lawyers, but he couldn't do it while maintaining the lifestyle he and his wife were accustomed to.

Once he was convinced that that change was really important to him, we worked on the best way to tell his partner so that the change he desired wouldn't cause conflict between them. When the time came, he summoned all his courage and told her. He went straight to the point ("I want to do this"), and though he was ready to unleash the whole arsenal of arguments he had prepared to combat her objections, she stopped him and asked him just one question: "Will this make you happy?". When he replied that it would, she said that was all she needed to know. That night over dinner, they were both full of excitement about the new project.

He had spent years not saying anything out of a fear of something (her rejection) that never happened.

If what you need, if what you want, is right and good and you don't go for it, you have to ask yourself what you're so afraid of. Because you might be losing out on opportunities due to fears that are more present in your head than they are in reality.

Relationships with authority

To live in peace, you have to reclaim your own freedom, which doesn't mean living outside the social organization that sustains you: it means finding the balance between your individual freedom and respect for authority.

Every civilization has its powerful figures, charged with preserving the community through compliance with laws.

However, power corrupts and it makes those who enjoy it believe they deserve privileges. The difficult task of keeping people in line can lead to the abuses of power we know exist and that happen at every single social level, from families to work unions and including religious communities.

In situations of abuses of power, the worst thing is not what the powerful person does, but what they force others to do. If submitting to authority creates problems of integrity for you, it's time to analyze what's going on and what you can do to rebalance things.

In our society, I'm convinced that we can aspire to something better than acting out of fear of our leaders rather than out of personal responsibility. History has taught us that collective wellbeing, progress and peace can be achieved in communities whose members treat each other with respect much more than in communities where people are made to submit to authority under fear of reprisals. At the end of the day, authority and authoritarianism are not the same thing.

Summary:

–   If what you need or want is fair but is not aligned with your interests or you don't dare to go after it, you have to ask yourself what is holding you back: you may be missing out on opportunities due to fears that exist more in your head than in the real world.

–   To live in peace, you need to find a balance between your individual freedom and respect for rules.

–   We should live as organized beings, not subjugated ones.

–   History has shown that progress and peace are achieved in communities whose members treat each other with respect much more than in societies where punishment is fostered and the strongest people lay down the law.

Daily exercise:

<u>YOU ALREADY HAVE THE "NO"</u>

1. It's common to miss out on opportunities of all kinds because of a fear of "no". This exercise is going to expose you to that "no" by asking for small favors from people around you. For example, you can ask a neighbor for a cup of rice, a stranger for street directions, or a waiter for something not on the menu. The aim is not to put anyone out, but to observe your own emotions when you face your fear of "no".

2. You will see that most of the time, you get a "yes", and on few occasions you'll hear "no". Reflect on whether it was worth daring to ask.

3. With practice, you'll begin to know and be able to manage your own everyday fears, and you'll be more aware of your relationship with the rules. This will allow you to modify your behavior if necessary, in order to make you feel better.

Living with goals

I'm going to take advantage of the fact we spent yesterday looking at fear to continue looking at things that stop you from having goals.

Why do we need goals?

Life is action. Loving yourself means making the most of the time you have to do things that are worth doing.

The biggest sources of happiness come from the good results of your own actions. To achieve this, you need to have life goals, purposes, aims that inspire you.

Nathaniel Branden, a pioneer in the study of self-esteem, stated that one of his fundamental pillars was living with purpose: in other words, filling your life with meaning. And your life purpose doesn't have to be hugely important to mankind: it just has to make sense to you.

What is a life purpose?

Life purposes (or meanings, or profound motivations) are the ultimate reasons you live for. They are the voluntary personal missions that help you know who you are and what you want your place in the world to be. They guide your decisions and they cannot be imposed on you by other people.

If you want to be proud of yourself, if you want to go to bed each night full of hope, find goals. Picture yourself in a year's time, or ten years' time. Picture yourself as a happy ninety-year-old. Why would you be happy? What would that old man or woman have achieved in those ninety years?

We all have something we profoundly desire. Something we like to do, that we could do for hours. When we can, we make that our life's work. Sometimes, it just has to be something that accompanies us in our free time.

Do you know what you're good at or what you most desire? Is it close to being a purpose in your life? Bear in mind that doing something you love is reason enough to do it, regardless of the results.

Have a good plan

Do you have plans? Do you keep to them? Do they tend to turn out well?

I'm asking because I used to act without a plan. Not because I believed I didn't need one, but because I didn't know how to make one. I was overwhelmed by everything I had to organize in advance, I got impatient, I wanted to skip processes and I always ended up back where I started, or worse.

Then I learned how to draw up an efficient plan. And that made all the difference, enabling me to achieve more things with less effort, and my sense of satisfaction was greater.

That's why I invite you to spend some real time drawing up a plan to achieve the goals you set for yourself.

What should a good plan include?

1. Whatever you're trying to improve or achieve in the form of concrete objectives (don't just write "travel"; include specific goals).

2. Potential obstacles (and their solutions, if you know them. You can note them down as and when you encounter them).

3.   Balancing entries: the things you will have to give up for as long as your plan is in action, or permanently.

4.   Everything you're going to do to achieve this: new habits, routines, dates, changes to your spending dynamic, improvements to your self-care...

5.   All the answers to all the questions you can foresee right now.

Don't hesitate to seek advice when designing your plan, and ask for feedback. There are tons of professionals who can help you.

Immediately structure that information to turn it into a series of steps. Something like this:

1.   Define the goal.

2.   Define your values, virtues and strengths in relation to that goal.

3.   Figure out the exact point you're starting from right now.

4.   Note down everything achieving that goal will involve.

5.   Order what you wrote for the previous point and note down time frames for each step.

6.   Set yourself a start date and an approximate end date.

I advise you to write it neatly, using notes, colors or whatever else you need to make it understandable. You can use a journal, board, collection of Post-It notes or any other format you find effective[9].

We end today with a quote from Jim Rohn:

"I find it fascinating that most people plan their vacations with better care than they plan

---

9 I go into depth on this topic in the book *The Power of Goals*: www.danieljmartin.es/pog

their lives. Perhaps that is because escape is easier than change."

Summary:

-   It's not possible to lead a full and happy life without having clear life purposes: those ultimate reasons you get out of bed in the morning.

-   The greatest sources of happiness are the good results of your own actions.

-   We all have something we deeply desire. Something we like to do and can do for hours. We should try never to let it leave our lives.

-   Your goals will be much easier to achieve if you have a realistic plan for reaching them.

Daily exercise:

YOUR LIFE PURPOSES

1.   Based on what we've done today, decide what your life purposes are (two to four of them). For example: to create a happy home, to make your mark on your profession, to be the best mother or father you can be, to explore your limits at a certain activity or vocation, and so on.

2.   Ask yourself if your everyday life is aligned with those purposes. If it's not, what should you do to make it so?

3.   Draw up an action plan for each of those purposes and follow it. Remember you can change your route, but you can't stop.

DAY 19

Leave procrastination for tomorrow

If you want to fight for your dreams and goals, there's something you need to get rid of: damn procrastination. We all know how useless and harmful it is, so why do we always slip back into it?

Let's look at it in a little more depth.

We constantly see last-minute offers and commercials saying things like: Last days at this price! You're just in time: a few spaces left! Last few tickets! In movies, the hero always deactivates the bomb at the last second. In rom-coms, the protagonists realize they're in love right at the end, when one of them races to stop the other from getting on a plane. It seems like everything that happens at the last moment is more valuable, more authentic! Why not leave things to the last minute in our lives, too?

Procrastination is a waste of time and energy and it subjects you to a rollercoaster of emotions: you go up with the false sense of satisfaction that you're "cheating time" when you put a task off, then you get nervous when you realize it's catching up with you, then you drop down to guilt, anxiety and shame as you desperately battle against the clock and eventually reach euphoria when you manage to finish in time.

Procrastination is mentally exhausting and it creates a feedback loop: the more tired you are, the more tempting it is to leave things to the last minute, which makes you even more stressed and tired. Every minute of "pleasure" from procrastinating is paid with far more minutes of stress.

On the other hand, procrastination indicates a low level of commitment: it's like saying, underneath it all, you don't mind doing things by halves or even badly instead of doing them well. But why would we prefer to do things badly?

The answer is hidden somewhere in our brains. There is a voice in there that congratulates you for not doing things as well as you could have. It's like a sensation of superiority or rebellion against the norm. You don't go grocery shopping when you should because you're *more important* than that. You're not like other people.

Have you ever felt that way?

Boring obligations, especially household chores or things that everyone on the planet has to do and which therefore don't feel special, are the perfect target for procrastination. Because, I mean, what great genius or entrepreneur wastes time on such frivolous things as having clean socks every morning?

But you are not the laundry, or the dishwasher, or the mountain of paperwork you have to submit to the taxman: you are your habits, and your habits are to be an organized and responsible person.

At the other extreme, procrastination also happens when we spend way too much time prepping for a task. Need to send emails to new clients? No problem, but first let me clean my computer screen, it's dirty. Actually, I'd better clean my whole desk. Wait, I'll sweep the floor too, since I'm here. Oh, and I need to call the courier service. What time is it? Whoa, too late to start sending emails now. I'll just do it tomorrow.

Does this loop resonate with you? When you catch yourself saying these kinds of things, break the cycle and start working without listening to your brain: procrastination has taken it hostage.

The Ten Commandments of time management

To combat procrastination, here are my Ten Commandments of time management:

1.   Thou shalt use your diary every day: every night, plan the following day, and every morning check the task list for that day.

2.   Thou shalt consider your long-term agenda, the one with your life goals.

3.   Thou shalt plan each week, each month and each year when it begins.

4.   Thou shalt ask yourself frequently: what is the most important thing I need to do right now?

5.   Thou shalt fight in equal amounts against perfectionism and procrastination.

6.   Thou shalt learn to set limits on others' demands and on social pressures.

7.   Thou shalt not give your time to those who don't deserve it.

8. Thou shalt keep time-wasting activities under control.

9. Thou shalt learn to do what you can already do, but faster.

10. Thou shalt battle against Parkinson's Law[10].

10 Parkinson's Law (Cyril Northcote Parkinson, 1957) states that a task will take all the time available for it, even if it could be done in less time.

Summary:

–   Procrastination is normally fear: fear of failure and fear of success.

–   Sometimes, procrastination is born of a false sense of rebellion. In truth, it's just a lack of respect for yourself.

–   Planning, commitment and rewards are your best weapons against procrastination.

–   It's common to have great intentions, a lot of motivation and some amazing goals, but such bad time management that it ends up sinking every project you begin.

Daily exercise:

YOUR AGENDA AT THE HELM

1.   Find an agenda you like and that's easy to use. It can be a phone or computer app or, even better, a physical paper agenda.

2.   Use it every night and every morning, as well as every time you have a new task or commitment.

3.   In time, you'll notice whether you're using it for a daily to-do list or to plan your tasks according to your goals. If you only use it to remind you of medical appointments and birthday parties, you're not making the most of its potential, which is to organize your time around your goals. If that's you, train yourself to put your agenda at the helm of your life, rather than using it as a list of reminders.

The influence of your surroundings

It's been proven that behavior is contagious. The people you interact with, your workspace, your places of leisure, your family relationships: it all contributes to creating a favorable or unfavorable environment for your personal growth. It's no coincidence that many people adopt lifestyles similar to those of their parents, nor that in certain societies one certain work culture or way of thinking prevails.

Your actions are linked to your surroundings in the same way that your education comes from a certain environment. And I don't just mean the education you receive at home or school: if a teenager sees three betting houses on their way home from school, they are more likely to start gambling than one who sees none.

If you grow up in a family that doesn't value effort, it's likely that in the future you'll look for jobs or relationships that require minimal effort. On the other hand, if your friendship group has a mutually supportive dynamic where you find rewarding activities that help you grow, that will become a very important pillar in building healthy self-esteem.

It's true that some people achieve amazing success despite growing up in toxic environments (we've all heard of cases of celebrities from poor or dysfunctional families), but they tend to be the exception: statistics indicate the opposite usually happens.

Learn to use criticism

Something else that can strongly influence us is criticism (good or bad).

To avoid getting disheartened, people tend to be encouraged to ignore criticism, but I don't subscribe to that: I believe that you can use criticism to your own benefit.

It's true that many people criticize in order to hurt, invalidate or sabotage. But in life, we also receive a lot of potentially useful criticism. That's why it's important to learn how to manage it.

In addition, as Aristotle said, there is only one way to avoid criticism, and that's to do nothing, say nothing and be nothing. And that's not what you bought this book for, right?

When you accept that you will be criticized no matter what you do, you free yourself of the pressure to please others and of the fear of disappointing people: both those things will happen either way.

The criticism that damaged your self-esteem in the past was often an indicator you were on the right track: a track others secretly wanted to take themselves.

The more criticism you receive, the greater the proof you're making waves and aiming high enough to awaken others' envy. Don't let that criticism stop you. Or do you think that anyone is going to take their time to undermine your confidence if your success poses no threat to them? Just worry about keeping your own conscious clean and honest, and let them talk.

We encourage and praise our friends and loved ones for fighting to get to where we are, but it makes us uncomfortable if they go one step further. Keep this phrase in mind: "You will never be criticized by someone who's doing more than you, only by people who are doing less or nothing."

How to identify valuable criticism

Listen to all of it carefully and identify the observations that are true, in other words, that don't just annoy you but rather light a little lightbulb in your head: generally, that criticism comes from people who know about the topic and who don't see you as a threat but as someone doing something interesting, or someone with potential and passion who is not aiming at the right place yet. That tends to be the good criticism.

Embrace your sense of humor

If it were a food, I think humor would be a fruit with tons of antioxidants: laughter can rejuvenate us and improve our outlook on the world.

A sense of humor is often confused with sarcasm. The difference is your attitude: a sense of humor is taking pleasure in life's ability to surprise you. Sarcasm is a defense mechanism to avoid feeling vulnerable when faced with an aspect of life that intimidates you.

A sense of humor also tackles you as a person: laughing at your own setbacks involves relativizing your problems and taking your imperfections with wisdom. Don't mistake it for self-humiliation, because it's very different: people who denigrate themselves through "jokes" are just trying to get approval at the cost of their own dignity.

There are days when it's impossible to find even one moment of fun. But having bad days is not the same as having a bad life. Being able to joke is to connect with the lighter side of life and with the child you once were. So whenever you can, look for the funny side!

Summary:

–   Behavior is contagious.

–   Your actions are linked to your surroundings and your education comes from a certain environment.

–   If your environment is undermining your self-esteem or desire to grow, you need to go someplace else.

–   Don't be influenced by criticism: you need to consciously decide what needs to be listened to and what does not

–   You'll be happier if you keep a sense of humor (without being cynical, sarcastic or self-humiliating).

Daily exercise:

A GOOD INFLUENCE

1.   I've already mentioned that your actions will be influenced by your surroundings, not just in terms of people but also places. In this sense, do you think your house, the place where you live, is a good influence on you?

2.   Review how your living space is organized and decide whether it's a good or bad influence on your activities and goals, and how you can improve on it.

3.   Without getting into a lot of expense, make the changes you think you need to in order for your home to help your wellbeing, rest, productivity if you work from home, and so on. You will immediately see that your mood and motivation improve significantly.

Excuses!

Jim Rohn said: "If you really want to do something, you'll find a way. If you don't, you'll find an excuse."

We all invent excuses to get out of doing things we don't want or to excuse ourselves for something we did wrong. It's inevitable in a society that continuously demands that we give others our time. But the quantity of excuses we use says a lot about us: how reliable we are and whether our lives are more or less aligned with our goals.

We're not always aware that we're using excuses. That's why I'm about to give you a list of the main excuses my patients use for not taking action. I'm sure many of them will resonate with you:

The past

It's true that a lot of people get dealt bad hands in life. If that's you, remember that taking action will help you. You may not be able to battle on every front you would like to, but don't stop fighting: you'll see that life will come around. Remember that you are not your past, and your past does not determine your future.

The world is going to hell

Unlike the previous one, this excuse doesn't tend to be used by people who have been unlucky but rather by those who have a more luxurious comfort zone. Complaining about the government, about the way people behave, about the times we live in, about world hunger, and so on, is valid, but not doing anything because "it's not worth it" is not. Once you refine your observational skills, you will realize that those who complain the most about the way the world is going are those who least contribute to improving it. If you're one of those people, consider the extent to which you're part of the problem rather than the solution.

I'm not ready

This is very laudable when it's genuine. If you don't feel ready for a relationship, a more ambitious job or a marathon, it's better for you to say so. However, if you really want something, set a date and detail the requirements to be ready for it. If you don't, you're in excuse mode.

It won't work

People who use this excuse are experts in ruining their own dreams and those of others. Under the guise of "being realistic", they sink amazing projects before even beginning them. Yes, you need to keep your feet on the ground, but not to live paralyzed because you already think something won't work. You can't read the future!

"It won't work" is a self-fulfilling prophesy. This self-fulfilling prophesy is a defense mechanism, more or less consciously, that we use to make something fail just like we "predicted" it would. The problem is that that prediction is not based on objective fact but rather on distorted interpretations and intentions or ones which are outright made up.

I'm not good at it / It's not my thing

Statements like "I'm really bad at..." or "I'm useless at..." sometimes speak to our beliefs about our own abilities, but usually they are just excuses not to try something.

I already tried

It's true that failure is demoralizing. If you already tried something and failed, maybe you should just leave it, right? Well, no: picking your battles is wise, but not picking any is to underestimate yourself.

Before giving in, take that failure that hurt you to the autopsy room and analyze what went wrong. Then, assess the relationship between that failure and what you want to do today. If the goal is the same (like running a marathon), learn from experience and tackle it more effectively next time. Remember the quote from the beginning of this chapter: you have to keep on trying.

It's too late

Yes, time passes. You're no longer that spring chicken full of energy and passion who could take on the world. Your train has left the station, and you have to accept that. Is that what you think? Well, don't! It's never too late to start being who you want to be.

Behind many excuses lies paralyzing fear. It's risky to take a leap, but you have to try. Don't always believe that it's "better the devil you know" – in fact, try never to believe that.

"Don't say 'if I could, I would'. Say 'if I can, I will'."

— Jim Rohn

Summary:

- Behind most excuses lies a profound fear of change.

- It's unavoidable to make excuses sometimes so you don't give all your time to others.

- The number of excuses you use says a lot about you: how reliable you are and whether or not you lead a life more or less aligned with your own objectives.

Daily exercise:

THE EXCUSE DETECTOR

1.   The better you know yourself, the harder you will find it to make excuses and let yourself down. For example: if you hate going to the dentist, you might find that – somewhat subconsciously – you always find a reason to cancel or postpone your appointments. Now, I recommend that you detect the excuses you have used recently to get out of your obligations.

2.   Detect whether those excuses were for others (to get out of a party, to say no to a request, etc.), or to lie to yourself. The former gets a pass if only used occasionally, but the latter type should not exist in your life.

3.   Reflect on this type and find alternatives. It's not about always fulfilling your obligations to perfection every time, but about recognizing when you're just not prepared to do something.

Never give up

Life can be hard, and sometimes you might feel like abandoning your goals or objectives. If you get demotivated easily, if you make excuses, if you give up before making it, if you lack willpower... you should know you can get better with practice.

The willpower to do things with a distant reward leans on motivation itself, but there are things that can strengthen it. Here are eight of them:

1. **Talk to your temptation when it comes**. Treat it like an annoying salesman you need to get rid of politely: "I love the thing you're

selling, but I've already decided not to buy any more", "Yes, I know how good that makes me feel, but I also know how good it will feel to stick to what I've decided".

2. **Talk to yourself (respectfully) when you feel like giving up**. Talk to yourself the way you would a friend, or write yourself a letter. What would you say to yourself if you were someone else?

3. **Give your word.** Find someone you would hate to disappoint and promise them you'll achieve a certain thing. Keeping your word is comforting and it strengthens your confidence.

4. **Put money down.** Decide on an amount of money it would hurt to lose and give it up every time you fail. Give it to an organization, celebrity, sports team or political party you can't stand.

5. **Break it down.** If you have a task you don't want to do but that you know will benefit you, divide it up into stages and intersperse them with fun activities, or show your progress in a

quantifiable way and give yourself little rewards when you "move up a level".

6. **Keep it at bay.** Get rid of anything that might present a temptation: don't go to the mall to eat if you know you can't control your spending, ask a friend to look after your console for you for a week if your willpower can't take seeing it in your lounge.

7. **Don't fall down twice in a row.** If you skip a day on something for some reason, don't let it happen again right away. For example, if you skip a workout out of laziness, don't let yourself skip the next one.

8. **Picture your worst self.** Instead of visualizing the achievements you want, picture yourself wasting time, money or energy. For example: imagine yourself lying on the couch all day without lifting a finger, or losing your nerve in a delicate situation... Picture yourself doing the opposite of what would make you proud.

Choose your hard

We end today on a technique known as "choose your hard". It consists of selecting one of two "hard" options when faced with a situation, challenge or circumstance. Here are some examples:

– Watching what you eat and dieting is hard. Dealing with future health problems when you can't turn back time is hard. Choose your hard.

– Maintaining a relationship is hard. Being alone at the worst and best moments of your life is hard. Choose your hard.

– Having the discipline to practice for an hour every day is hard. Realizing in time that you never learned to play guitar and you only ever talked about it is hard. Choose your hard.

If you get used to testing your "dilemmas" in this way, many of your problems will quickly disappear (they actually haven't, but you will no longer see them as problems), and many dilemmas will stop being dilemmas because you will see some battles are better lost.

The fear of being better

We know that fear is the worry that the new and unknown will bring us unfavorable results. Our most primitive brain has taken thousands of years to train for survival, and it follows a strict anti-change policy when the situation is going remotely well. We understand this logic in shielding us from failure but... does it also shield us from success?

When you improve in any area, imposter syndrome often arises.

Imposter syndrome is the fear of being accused of being a fraud or liar by those around us (colleagues, friends...) because we don't believe in our own worth. As a defense mechanism, our brains anticipate that by making us feel unworthy of what we have achieved in order to protect us from something worse: the pain or shame of being "found out" or rejecting for occupying a place we don't truly *deserve*.

Imposter syndrome is a false belief linked to low self-esteem: we don't believe we're worth as much or don't think we deserve others' confidence in the job we're doing (not just professionally, but in relationships, too). To free yourself of this syndrome, you need to work on your self-esteem and show yourself with proof, no matter how small, that you are worth it and you do deserve people's trust.

Along with imposter syndrome, there is a fear of being abandoned by our group if our growth generates jealousy or envy. Unfortunately, there is something behind this fear: in fact, it's likely that improving yourself will cause a stir in your friendship group, family or relationship. However, and you should be very clear on this, that should not be your problem.

Don't waste time on trying to convince anyone that, despite your personal or professional growth, you're still worthy of their love or trust: those who care about you will still be by your side, and those who don't won't stay there no matter how many times you lend them a hand at your own expense.

Summary:

– We often consider abandoning our challenges, giving in or getting demotivated. To avoid this, feed and train your willpower.

– Changing tack might be necessary, but giving up is not an option.

– The fear of improvement (and so-called "imposter syndrome") can be as paralyzing as the fear of failure.

– When you feel demotivated, use the "choose your hard" technique.

Daily exercise:

<u>DON'T GIVE UP NOW!</u>

1.   Get a wall calendar or similar (any calendar where you can write things down and keep it to hand) and note down every achievement you get, no matter how small. For example: if you find it hard to go to the gym, note down the days you go, if you find it hard to keep the house clean, note down the days you cleaned, if you can't quit videogames, write down the days you decide not to play.

2.   Every so often, check your calendar and draw conclusions: is it worth giving in after all those achievements and all that effort? Wouldn't you be letting yourself down if you quit now?

3.   The aim of this exercise is to reinforce your willpower with real proof of everything you achieve.

DAY 23

Practice integrity

What is integrity and why is it essential to loving yourself?

Personal integrity is when your actions correspond to your values and convictions. When what you say, do and think all coincide. In other words: when you're true to yourself.

When your behavior aligns with your system of values, you feel good. When you stop being consistent (you betray yourself), internal discomfort begins: your own conscience lets you know that something doesn't tally.

If you're committed to your job, you will act accordingly: you will take your tasks seriously, be honest and feel good about it. If you don't, you feel like you sold out.

When I say that happiness depends on personal integrity, I mean that we often look for happiness in things that are not present in our system of values. I don't mean they are bad things, just that they are not essential for our fulfilment.

The more your life is aligned with the way you believe you should be living, the more you will enjoy it: personal integrity will feed your self-esteem.

It's true that having integrity won't guarantee your happiness, but not having it will guarantee your eternal unhappiness.

Choose empathy

Empathy is what sets us apart not from animals, but from psychopaths[11].

Empathy is the ability to respect and emotionally understand others. That doesn't mean knowing every detail of what's happening to someone, but rather seeing them as an equal who we should not ignore or harm. Empathy breeds solidarity, tolerance, support, generosity, and more.

Empathy is why the world is still spinning. Practicing empathy allows you to create stronger bonds with people, feel better about yourself, contribute to a reduction in violence, defend justice and foster emotional intelligence.

---

11 Psychopaths lack this ability: they can simulate empathy, but not feel it. Nor can they feel affection, solidarity or remorse.

How can you be more empathetic? Try these 5 strategies:

1.   **Practice active listening:** This involves listening attentively, without harassing and with the offer of sincere feedback.

2.   **Live without prejudice:** Live and let live. Don't judge, don't try to impose your truth. People have their own reasons for acting how they do, whether they are right or not. You will have time, if necessary, to confront things.

3.   **Communicate assertively without being intimidating:** Don't be impatient or aggressive in a disagreement unless someone is disrespecting you.

4. **Ask about what you don't understand**: Before drawing conclusions based on how things seem, ask about what you didn't understand. No one ever died because they asked a question, and it will save you endless misunderstandings and disappointments.

5. **Observe:** When you're observant, you catch expressions and gestures that tend to go unnoticed and which will help you to understand others. Remember that not everyone thinks like you or needs the same things you do.

Remember this:

"Everyone you meet is fighting a battle you know nothing about. Be kind. Always."

— Robin Williams

Differences, welcome!

Judging by the number of self-help books that pass through my hands, it seems like there are only neurotypical people in this world. Specifically, middle-class western people of standard intelligence who can easily adapt to the predominantly masculine societal model. Others, people with different traits, should accept their "limitations" and live their lives asking for permission or forgiveness.

Not only is this belief unfair, it's also totally false: it takes all sorts to make a world.

In terms of intelligence, until very recently people were divided into having "normal" cognitive capacity (neurotypical) or with "faults" in their systems, for want of a better term. Fortunately, nowadays science offers a much fairer and more realistic view of neurodiversity.

What are neurodivergent people?

Neurodivergent people are those with ASD (Autistic Spectrum Disorder), ADHD (Attention Deficit/Hyperactive Disorder), dyslexia, dyspraxia, OCD (Obsessive-Compulsive Disorder), dyscalculia, bipolar disorder, Tourette's syndrome, and others, in addition to non-neurotypical conditions such as Down's Syndrome or sensorial disabilities.

Put simply: millions!

While it's true that western society is increasingly inclusive, our production systems are less so. Why is this? Well, some people believe it is better to keep those "profiles" away from the world of work, in case they end up occupying... you know, positions of responsibility.

Leaving aside the ethical considerations, discounting a neurodivergent person from a production system is not only unfair, it's a mistake, since such people often offer some advantages over "normative" brains.

For example, there is evidence that people with ASD are more creative than the average neurotypical person. That doesn't mean that they're good at drawing (although they may be), but rather that they find different solutions to problems because they use diagonal thinking. Many people with autism are very skilled at calculus, detecting patterns or data management[12].

To love ourselves like we all deserve, no one should feel invalidated because of their neurodivergence or disability.

"Everybody is a genius. But if you judge a fish on its ability to climb a tree, it will live its whole life believing it is stupid."

— Albert Einstein

---

[12] Note: I omitted the ethical considerations here only to focus on the benefits of diversity in production systems.

Summary:

– Personal integrity is when our actions correspond to our values and convictions. In other words: when we're true to ourselves.

– There can be no happiness or self-esteem when we feel that we are not doing the right thing according to who we are or want to be.

– Empathy keeps the world turning. Practicing empathy allows you to create stronger bonds with people, contribute to reducing violence, defend justice and foster emotional intelligence.

– The world belongs to all of us; it's not for use exclusively by "normal" people.

Daily exercise:

IS YOUR SYSTEM OF VALUES SOLID?

1.   We've talked about how integrity involves acting according to your own values and principles. However, sometimes you don't know what those are until a specific situation forces you to look at them. It's common in such cases to make an impulsive decision or get swept up by the majority. That's why it's important to be clear on your values from the start.

2.   I invite you to reflect on the following situation: someone has sent to a WhatsApp group you're in an unfortunate photo of a woman you know. The photo is actually pretty funny and it gives rise to all kinds of jokes and comments. What do you do? What do you gain or lose by doing that?

3.   Reflect on the decision you've made and on how that makes you feel.

The dark side of money

They say that the path to corruption is the combination of a favorable environment, an opportunity and a type of person. If you can't avoid the first two factors (the environment and the opportunity), avoid the third: don't become the type of person who gets corrupted by money.

Compromising your honesty in order to get more money than you're owed is to feed your narcissism and emotional coldness. Look at it this way: how would you feel if you heard that some sons of bitches had scammed an old blind lady by telling her they were from the bank? I'm guessing you would feel rage and disgust. However, if you cheat too (you know: paying for or doing work under the table, concealing information to get welfare, inflating invoices, "forgetting" to pay for things, scamming, stealing, and so on) then you are contributing to an environment where others end up stealing from vulnerable people. Where is the limit?

If you take one small step toward corruption, someone else will feel justified in taking one step more. And the next person will feel justified in stealing from your parents or your children. Staying above reproach is the right thing to do.

Stop wanting things

"Love people, use things." [13] It goes that way round, not the other.

We live in a spiral of consumerism where we are basically working in order to acquire things.

---

13 This is a quote from the minimalists Joshua Fields and Ryan Nicodemus, and it's also the title of their first book.

And while, on the one hand, millions of people struggle to reach the end of the month, on the other hand at no point in human history have we had so many thousands of objects and services at our disposal.

I believe we urgently need reeducation in order to live with fewer material needs and more meaning. I'm not saying we should all take a poverty vow. I'm saying that you shouldn't value your worth by the money you have, nor expect others to do the same. Money works for us, not the other way around, and it's the route to doing wonderful things, not a way to accumulate useless crap in your garage.

How to buy beyond what's necessary

Are you someone who can't stop buying stuff or making lists of what you're going to buy soon? Here are some tips about consumerism, inspired by minimalism:

–   Before buying something, wait for its price in hours: if it costs fifty dollars, wait fifty hours before buying it. If it costs a thousand dollars, wait a thousand hours.

–   Give the three R's a chance: reduce, reuse and recycle.

–   Make sensible shopping lists and stick to them.

–   If something comes into your house, something else needs to go out.

–   Cancel your subscriptions to services and stores to stop marketing emails.

–   Stop going onto online shopping websites just to "see what's new".

–   Sales: were you going to buy that thing before you saw it on sale?

–   Buy thinking about yourself, not others. This goes for a purse to impress your colleagues and for a guitar in the same model as your favorite guitar player – who, by the way, is a millionaire.

– Work out the price of the thing you want in hours of work. How much time do you have to work in order to buy it?

– Parties, birthdays, celebrations, Christmas: negotiate with your family and friends to limit spending or agree to give more conscious gifts rather than gifting for the sake of it.

– Vacations and leisure: before booking your next trip to the latest fashionable destination, remember what vacations are for and what you hope to gain from your next travel adventure.

– Be materialistic, but by valuing each object for exactly what it is; don't give it "magical powers".

Forget advertising

I have several publicist friends and my tirades against advertising make them nervous. Not because I'm revealing any unutterable secrets (or am I?), but because what I say attacks the cornerstone of their trade:

Advertising is bullshit.

I'm not saying that advertising doesn't *sell* real things: cars, watches, clothes, perfume. I'm saying that what surrounds those items, that promise is a more exciting, desirable or authentic life: that part is pure bullshit.

Advertising does not aspire to leave consumers satisfied: quite the opposite. It is a potent generator of anxiety and frustration. Why? Because what it promises is an illusion. Of course, a nice perfume will make you smell good, and a good car is better than a bad one. But they won't turn you into a new person, nor can they stop time, nor can they transform your life into a dream.

To avoid the frustration the siren call of advertising leads to, my advice is to buy the products that make you happy, to try things out, to change brand if you want to (you don't owe anything to any company), but keep your expectations in the real world. The most a perfume is going to do for you is make you smell good. The rest is up to you.

> *"We spend money we do not have, on things we do not need, to impress people who do not care."*
>
> — Will Smith

Summary:

–   Compromising your honesty to get more money than you are owed feeds narcissism and emotional coldness.

–   Don't let money corrupt you; it's not worth it.

–   Every has to find a way to relate to money without dedicating their lives to working to buy things in order to be respected or calm their anxieties.

–   Advertising generates frustration because it promises impossible things and keeps you always wanting something more.

Daily exercise:

THE ASSET MANAGER

1.   Imagine that you have to take charge of your best friend's assets, consisting of their house, car, monthly salary and savings.

2.   Think about how you would do it, what things you would buy them, what you would get rid of and how much you would save every month for your friend. Does it coincide with what you would do if they were your own finances? Would you be more scrupulous, or less? Would you be able to easily explain to your friend how you were spending their money?

3. Take into consideration the various differences you see and make the changes you think are necessary in the way you manage your money.

The value of communication

We've already talked about active listening and the ability to defend your own boundaries. Success in these areas comes from assertive communication: knowing how to present your own interests effectively, without disrespecting yourself or anyone else.

Today, we will talk about how to communicate correctly. These are the resources to bear in mind:

— Express yourself clearly and directly. That doesn't mean being rude or aggressive: you can be both polite and firm.

– Avoid ambiguity, insinuation and over-explanation.

– If you're nervous when expressing yourself in certain settings, begin by expressing desires and opinions on unimportant topics and expose yourself to increasingly more significant situations as your confidence grows.

– Say "no" more often.

– Reduce phrases like "whatever you want", "it's fine by me", "I don't mind", and so on.

– Avoid giving too many explanations when a decision only affects you.

– Talk in the first person when expressing an opinion or complaint: "I think that...", "my opinion is..." and so on.

– Avoid apologizing when expressing a need or want that does not infringe on anyone else's rights.

–   Watch your body language and tone of voice: talk calmly, without raising your voice, but without hiding. Look the other person in the eyes.

–   Understand that in life, conflict will arise that you need to face, even if it makes you uncomfortable. Don't always keep quiet.

–   Be persistent when you know you're in the right.

–   Try not to go on the defensive or be aggressive.

–   Pick your battles. It's impossible to always be firm and achieve justice at every moment in life. Sometimes, you just have to let something go.

The result of an assertive action won't always be what you expect. Sometimes you have to insist, explain better, even concede. However, knowing how to communicate in the best possible way will save you a lot of time, energy and displeasure.

Share what you know

My patients are often reluctant to share the information or knowledge they possess. I understand that they don't have to tell anyone how much weight they lost if they don't want to, but they could share the phone number of the nutritionist who helped them.

My opinion is that sharing knowledge is a two-way street: if you do it, others will do it for you (not everyone, of course, but that will also help you to know who's on your team and who isn't). In addition, life is unexpected sometimes and you never know what doors it might open for you in the future.

Of course, if you have an amazing and achievable business idea, don't shout it from the rooftops: if you don't cover your back, someone might steal it from you. But don't be afraid to share your experience or information with others in your profession or talk about job offers, conferences, contacts... That will transmit the idea that you're not afraid of rivalry because you believe in yourself.

Summary:

– Effective communication saves a lot of time, energy and conflict.

– Expressing yourself clearly and directly doesn't mean being rude or aggressive.

– When you're presenting your own interests, needs and wants, be polite but firm.

– Sharing your knowledge in a safe environment is a positive thing and becomes a two-way street.

Daily exercise:

<u>WE HAVE TO TALK</u>

1.   I invite you to mentally practice assertive communication in the following situations:

-    You've landed your dream job, but it's in another city a hundred miles away. Tell your partner.

-    You don't want to carry on seeing someone casually. Tell the person you've been seeing for the past few weeks.

-    You need your sibling to lend you five thousand dollars.

-    You're annoyed that your partner is flirting with someone.

-    You suspect that your best friend's partner is cheating on them.

2.   Which did you find hardest? Why do you think that's the case? When might you end up conceding to the other person's response?

3.   The aim of this exercise is to train your assertive communication in situations where the other person is going to be mad, upset or betrayed.

Don't try to fix people

As Robin Williams said, everyone is fighting a battle they must face alone. Not because they can't trust others, but because no one can fix someone else, no matter how hard they might try.

Giving people advice and support is great, but it's delicate. Telling someone what they should do in order to heal is already harsh. I mean, do you like being given advice you didn't ask for? In addition, support should be to help the other person, but we often use it for our own vanity.

When should you NOT try to fix others' problems?

–   When they didn't ask for it.

–   When you do it expecting something in return.

–   When you do it to feed your ego and with the sole intention of coming off well.

–   When you insist and get frustrated if they don't listen to you, because you "know" you're right.

–   When you haven't put yourself in the other person's shoes.

–   When you only want to treat the symptoms, not the underlying problem.

People who devote themselves to fixing others have their own internal battles going on, but they're so fearful of them that they prefer to focus on others: deep down, they consider themselves to be a lost cause.

If you don't know what to say to someone else's troubles, just give them support with phrases such as:

- Is there anything I can do to help?

- I don't know what to say, but I'm with you on this.

- I don't fully understand the situation, but I'm here if you need me.

- What would help you to feel better?

Summary:

– We're often tempted to solve other people's problems because of our own vanity instead of through true solidarity.

– Helping someone through a specific time is not the same as trying to change them "for their own good".

– Before fixing someone else, make sure your own mind is in order.

Daily exercise:

<u>I KNOW WHAT'S BEST FOR YOU</u>

1.   You're worried because your sibling has been obsessed with losing weight for some time and you suspect they have developed an eating disorder.

2.   Imagine that you share your concern with them, but it doesn't make them change. Quite the opposite: they get mad at you and tell you to mind your own business. What do you do?

3.   Analyze how you would feel and what your reaction would be. Remember that your actions should seek to improve the situation, not demonstrate who is right.

Get the vampires out of your life

We're coming to the end of our bootcamp and it's time to tackle another big elephant in the room: your relationships with vampires.

Getting vampires out of your life is essential and non-negotiable. If you want to be the captain of your own freedom and future, those people need to leave your life right now. We've already talked about self-respect and personal boundaries. It's time to get the vampires out.

What are vampires? They are people who feed off your energy:

- Negative people.

- Liars.

- Envious people.

- Critical or gossipy people.

- Perpetual victims and complainers.

- Defiant, belligerent people.

- Manipulative people.

- Opportunists and schemers.

Yes, the world is full of people like them! But you don't have to let them into your house, and you certainly don't have to try and change them.

So, what should you do?

You can and should aspire to maintain a healthy relationship with everyone. Some of these relationships will be very close, others will be good working relationships, others simply cordial. But on every level, you want them to add, not take away.

When you encounter situations where you have to live with or deal with toxic people, you need to learn to manage them (not manipulate, which is something different). Here are some techniques that can be very useful:

— **Emotional distance:** Some of these people are great actors and actresses, and they play Oscar-worthy roles in order to get what they want. Be impassive when you detect such fakery, or even if their suffering is real, when they are insisting that it's your duty to help them.

— **Hold your tongue:** Don't offer unnecessary details about yourself to these people. Reduce interactions to neutral conversations and don't show your feelings or opinions on any topic that could become a weapon later.

- **Let them be right:** These people tend to be childish and spoiled, and they always need to be right and have the last word. Don't get bogged down in changing them; just let them be right. It's not very ethical, but it works.

- **Don't give them your time:** Try to always be busy for those people. Whether it's this prior arrangement or that issue, somehow the weeks fly by... and you didn't have time to meet up with them.

- **Become their vampire, too:** Ask them for favors, call them, ask them questions, beg them for love, insist on sharing everything with them, introduce them to your family, tell them you need to borrow money... they'll soon show themselves out.

- **Don't be alone with them:** These people tend to lie and twist things, and they're even good at insisting until they have bent you to their will. But if you have witnesses, they tend to shrink back.

The less time you spend with toxic people, the more time you will have for the people who are worth it. Remember that healthy relationships are established between people who respect each other, communicate mutually in a positive tone, support and encourage one another, and also lead free and independent lives.

Rather than seeking people "on your level", from your professional or social class, just surround yourself with good, loyal and positive people.

> *"Happy people don't waste time doing wrong by others. Evil is for people who are unhappy, frustrated, mediocre and envious."*
>
> — Robin Williams

Run from Job's friends!

Good friends are a treasure. Bad ones... not so much.

In the Old Testament, Job's friends were four men who went to encourage the prophet when he was going through the worst time of his life. However, instead of empathizing with his misfortune, they ended up blaming him for his own suffering: worst of all, they did it from a position of comfortable wealth and wellbeing, without really putting themselves in his shoes. Sound familiar to you?

Yes, Job's friends are essentially all useless friends. Those who "encourage" you by downplaying your problems or giving you impossible solutions.

The problem with these useless friends (or life coaches, or arrogant relatives, or bad therapists) is that sometimes their intentions are good, so it's hard to make them see that their advice isn't helping... at least, without them getting mad at you.

What do Job's friends tend to say?

– **They say:** "Cheer up!" when you're depressed, not understanding that an emotional down or depression is not a jacket you can take off when you get too hot.

– **They say:** "If it's bad for you, leave" without understanding the dynamics that keep someone in an abusive relationship or toxic behaviors.

– **They say:** "Forgive and forget", not realizing that an open wound requires more than just a cheerful clean slate.

The problem with Job's friends are not their "solutions" or advice. The problem is that, when they see those things aren't working, instead of reviewing their advice, they blame you: they say you're not trying hard enough, or that you like to play the victim, or that you're being immature. And I'm not saying that's never the case. But generally those are not the kinds of friends who will make you see it.

You need to get away from Job's friends, no matter how good they are as people. If you can't physically leave them, because they are family or other people you can't avoid, then you need to distance yourself emotionally: become impermeable to their advice and "encouragement".

A group is not a cult

Generally speaking, all groups are based on the following dynamic: the members accept a small amount of personal sacrifice or obedience to the established norms in return for a greater benefit. This could be pay, fun with friends, a partner's love...

But the equation should be this, and not the inverse: what you get should be bigger and better than what you give. If not, the relationship is corrupt.

When can you say that a relationship or group has become corrupted?

When one or more of the following situations arise:

–   When the group pushes you to do things you don't want.

–   When you can't explain why you're still there.

–   When there is a leader to whom you owe a great degree of loyalty.

–   When you're paying for things you didn't do.

–   When you or someone else feels humiliated.

–   When there is so much unpredictability that you're always on high alert.

–   When you always moderate your behavior and words in order to avoid arguments.

–   When you feel like you need permission to act.

–   When there are internal, almost secret, rules that no one outside that group would understand.

–   When those internal rules defy the law.

–   When you're never enough as you are.

–   When they lie to you or keep things from you.

–   When you feel you're either with them or against them.

Summary:

–   You need to distance yourself from fake friends, toxic people and "vampires" in general. If you can't do it physically, you should do it emotionally so that their toxic behavior can't upset you.

–   You have no moral obligation to "carry" any self-sufficient adult.

–   When an environment goes against your interests, it goes against you.

–   You're not obligated to accept, be grateful for or follow the advice anyone gives you.

Daily exercise:

A VAMPIRE-FREE ZONE

1.   Make a list of people who, one way or another, steal energy from you. They could be family members, colleagues, or friends.

2.   Write down exactly what bothers you about their behavior and what they should do so that it stops bothering you.

3.   Reflect on whether there is a real possibility your relationship with that vampire could become healthy. If it can't, get ready to distance yourself from that person in the way you consider most appropriate.

DAY 28

Your future will be okay

Does the thought of your future scare you? Yes?

I don't think it does. I think what scares you is repeating a past that was painful. And that's not going to happen, because you're already working on it.

There is reason to believe in a happy future, and there is reason for hope. Yes, the world is troubled, there is war, hunger, and violence... but there are also so many people (including you) who get out of bed every morning and make the world a little more human.

Let me tell you four things:

–   **One**: Even though the number of wars and war casualties is still unacceptable, they are falling: studies show there are increasingly fewer wars and conflict-related deaths in the world.

–   **Two**: Life expectancies are on the rise, and many diseases that used to kill millions of people are being eradicated thanks to dedicated people working in science and education.

–   **Three:** We are more aware of threats to our species and to the planet, and we are increasingly prepared to take them on.

–   **Four:** More and more generations are being educated about human rights, which will help build a more equal world.

Have intentions, not expectations

In the same way you have requirements when choosing a hotel or a degree, you need to have requirements for your life and your future.

Life requirements are everything you demand from your life. Sadly, they are not guaranteed in writing nor are there any refunds, so it's important to have intentions rather than expectations. Why? Because expectations are passive. They are wishes. Intentions drive you to act.

How can you achieve this?

By focusing on your actions, not on the results you want from them.

I invite you to reflect on your expectations in life. What are they? A good job? To start a family? To travel the world? To live a long time? A golden retirement? To go down in history for your achievements?

Now, I ask you to turn those expectations into intentions. What have you done today to achieve them? What will you do tomorrow?

You never stop getting to know yourself

There is no limit to knowing yourself; it's a process that will accompany you throughout your life, because at every stage, at every age, you can discover something you didn't know about your personality, your abilities or your desires.

So, how can you get to know yourself better as an adult?

It's true that most of our traits arise during our formative school years. But they don't stop there; it's just that as adults, we become less curious. That's why you should stoke your curiosity a little by keeping an open mind to new things and living with something of an adventurous spirit.

What can help you to get to know yourself a little better every day?

–   New activities (visiting places, trying food, meeting people...).

–   Learning new things, from languages and hobbies to the challenges the future poses.

–   Observing your daily life and identifying why you do the things you do.

–   Asking people who know you to describe you.

–   Listening to your inner discourse.

–   Observing how you act in new or exceptional situations so you can draw conclusions regarding the future.

Summary:

– Often, what scares us most about the future is that the past will repeat itself.

– There are reasons to want the future and reasons for you to want yours. Because it looks bright.

– Expectations, if they're not accompanied by intentions that will push you to act, are just coins in a wishing well.

– Accept every new discovery as a gift and don't be ashamed of what you don't know yet.

Daily exercise:

DESIGN YOUR VISION BOARD

1.   A vision board is a board with images and words that represent what you want to be, feel, do or have in your life. It's a visual statement of intent. Do you dare to design your own?

2.   You can draw it up yourself or hire a graphic designer. I'll give you the basic steps:

a)   Define your goals.

b)   Gather key words and images that relate to them.

c)   Do some composition tests (balance aesthetics with function).

d)   Choose a support to stick it to.

e)   Choose the best place to display your vision board.

3. Glance at your vision board every day. If you do, then every day you will consider your dreams for the future and your subconscious will automatically work on them.

Accept praise and celebrate achievement

Have you ever noticed how bad we are at accepting compliments? I see it with my girlfriend: whenever one of her friends tells her she loves her dress, or a client thanks her for her efficiency on a project, she downplays it by saying that the dress is old or cheap, or that she's only doing her job.

Why is it so hard for us to accept a compliment?

It's true that some flattery is inappropriate or leads to uncomfortable situations. Sometimes, we suspect that it has a hidden agenda. We think:

"Do they want something from me?", "Are they just hitting on me?", and so on.

I believe that if a compliment is polite, you have to accept it. Just like someone accused of a crime is presumed innocent, we should believe by default that a polite compliment is sincere. There will be time later to figure out if it was or not.

However, it's like being passed a hot potato! We tend to react badly to compliments because we don't know what to do with them. On the one hand, we don't want to appear vain or incite envy. On the other, we try to return the compliment straight away, which doesn't always sound genuine. Finally, and most importantly: it's our low self-esteem and imposter syndrome that replies for us. We think something like: "Oh, God! This person thinks I'm better than I am! What will they think when they *find out the truth*?".

The truth is that there is only one correct response to a compliment, and it's "thank you". That is what the other person deserves. You don't have to justify anything, you don't have to explain, you don't have to fire back another compliment. Just say thank you.

Any other response just says: "you're wrong", "I don't want your opinion", or "I don't deserve flattery". We want to protect ourselves, but all we do is devalue the other person and ourselves.

If someone praises something about you, it's because you deserved it. If they do it with an ulterior motive, that's their problem, not yours – and you'll discover it sooner or later.

Celebrate your achievements

From time to time, stop and celebrate how far you've come. Why? I'll give you a few reasons:

– Celebrating an achievement, triumph or success has a positive impact on your wellbeing and self-esteem, especially if you can record the moment with a picture to look back on when you're feeling low.

– Celebrating an achievement lets others know about it and gives you a chance to receive praise from others and also to inspire them, which is highly rewarding.

– Celebrating an achievement bolsters your confidence in the plans and strategies you have adopted.

– Celebrating achievements reinforces your social ties in a positive way, whether it's at work, in the family, with your partner or with your team.

– Celebrating achievements recharges your batteries after all that effort and gets you ready for your next action in a much more positive way than if your achievement went unnoticed.

– Celebrating small goals encourages you to strive for bigger challenges.

Not only should you celebrate your achievements, you should also celebrate the time you spent working on or involved in something, such as anniversaries with your partner or at your company.

It's also good to celebrate others' achievements: you have nothing to envy if you're working on being better every day (in fact, it's been proven that those who feel envy most intensely are those who are not doing anything to achieve their goals, while those who are doing their best tend not to be jealous of others' success).

And don't forget to celebrate your birthday, too. Turning a year old and being able to celebrate it with the people in your life is an achievement in itself, and it deserves to be marked and remembered.

How to celebrate an achievement

Abraham Joshua Heschel, a prominent Jewish theologian, said that people today have forgotten the original meaning of celebration. When we achieve something, we immediately reward ourselves with pleasurable material objects, when according to him, celebration should be a conscious act of reflection on what made that achievement possible and on our gratitude toward life. In his words, "celebration is a confrontation, giving attention to the transcendent meaning of one's actions."

That said, in my opinion it is also important to reward yourself with something real. I agree with moderating our spending and vacuous entertainment, but there's nothing wrong with having a good time or treating yourself occasionally, after completing a challenge you're proud of.

My advice: be aware of why you're giving yourself something and try to turn that something into a moment of happiness. If you buy yourself a new jacket, the gift is not the jacket, it's feeling good every time you put it on because you remember the effort that went into achieving that goal.

If you can't always buy stuff, how could you treat yourself?

Anything that gives you some healthy happiness for a while: a different kind of family gathering (there is life beyond meals that devolve into football talk or politics), a new experience, dinner at an exotic restaurant, concert tickets, a service that brings wellbeing, a break for some conscious rest, an item related to your hobbies, a sum of money earmarked for a trip. What matters is that you remember how you earned that reward.

Oh, and remember: if anyone asks, tell them the truth. "I promised myself I would buy it if I achieved a certain thing... and I did!". It's not about piquing envy, it's about not downplaying your accomplishments.

Summary:

–   There is only one correct response to a compliment, and it's "thank you".

–   When you downplay a compliment, you're telling the person "you're wrong", "I don't want your opinion", "I don't deserve flattery".

–   Celebrating an achievement bolsters your confidence.

–   You should celebrate your achievements, no matter how small, as well as the anniversary of anything that's important in your life.

Daily exercise:

BECAUSE I'M WORTH IT

1.   This famous L'Oréal slogan helps me to introduce the penultimate exercise in our bootcamp. Let's dedicate it to celebrating an achievement of yours.

2.   Think about a reward or gift you would like to give yourself. Then, think of an achievement or effort that would be worth that gift.

3.   Commit to getting it for yourself if you achieve the thing you suggested (only if you achieve it or consider you tried your very best). Once you do, pay attention to how it makes you feel. If you do this exercise frequently, you will feel much prouder of yourself and it will motivate you to keep making bigger changes with less effort.

Failure is not even trying

So, we've come to the final day of our bootcamp. And we're going to dedicate it to failure.

We often identify mistakes as failures and failure as the impossibility of feeling good about ourselves.

But making a mistake is not the same as failing. We have already established that the former is inevitable. The second is a defeat you don't get back up from. Actually, when my patients are mourning a failure, often all they have really done is make a mistake. Potentially a serious mistake, but nothing that can't be overcome.

The only failure is not even trying.

Trying to do what?

Trying to become better and happier.

You should believe in yourself. Have the confidence you had when you were two: you didn't even know how your hands worked, but you tried them anyway. You didn't think: "Hmm, I've never grabbed this object before. I'd better not try."

Didn't you learn to walk at barely over a year of age? Didn't you pass your exams? Haven't you made some great friends? You have achieved so many things in life. And you're going to achieve so many more. If you don't believe in yourself, show yourself all the proof you've been accumulating since you were born.

You can't guarantee you will never fail. But failing at something is not the same as being a failure. In addition, it helps you anticipate falls, plan things, and avoid acting blindly or impulsively.

Nothing is 100% certain, so in psychology we encourage taking action once you have a 75% chance of success. That 75% is enough to justify at attempt: that way, you prevent the need to be totally sure (which is impossible anyway) from becoming an eternal excuse for doing nothing.

Leave perfection to the gods

The flip side of failure is perfectionism. Because, when you obsess over perfection, any action with a result less than perfect is perceived as failure.

Phrased like that, it's very easy to interpret that, if we root the concept of perfection out of our lives, we also root out failure. But it's not that simple. Let's look at some practical examples:

Should your house be better? Cleaner, tidier, better maintained? What about the company you work for, could it function better? Does your diet need to improve? What about people in your city? Everyone should drive better, so first, the streets need to be cleaner...

Everything should be much better... but you're not a god. And this is coming from someone (me) who spends their life trying to make people be better. However, I focus on reinforcing the positives instead of getting bogged down by everything that's going wrong.

Most religions state that we are imperfect copies of a god or gods. How, then, are we supposed to achieve perfection? We can't! But we don't need to. Do you know why? Because even though we're imperfect, we are capable of amazing things. You yourself have done wonderful things over the course of your life so far: a cake, a job, a test, a presentation, a workout, an event... and to think you're imperfect!

If you were perfect, doing things perfectly would have no merit; it would be easy. The merit here is being imperfect and still doing amazing things: your move, gods!

Forget perfection and focus on excellence. They're similar, but not the same: while the quest for perfection stops you from enjoying things you're good at, excellence invites you to grow while enjoying every accomplishment you collect.

Behind excellence is a decision to work voluntarily in order to reach a goal that makes you happy. Behind perfectionism is self-punishment and a fear of failure.

Commit to excellence and try to make the best decisions you can with every step you take. That's enough.

"Trust yourself. You know more than you think you do."
— Benjamin Spock

Summary:

- The only failure is not even trying.

- On our deathbeds, we only regret two things: the things we didn't dare to attempt, and the mistakes we chose not to learn from.

- If you were perfect, doing things perfectly would have no merit.

- Perfection is for gods. Excellence is for us mortals.

Daily exercise:

<u>TAKE RISKS! LOVE! LIVE!</u>

1. Close your eyes and imagine you're on your deathbed, surrounded by loved ones. Think about all the things you wanted to do in your life and never dared to try out of a fear of failure: what places did you never visit? What people did you miss out on meeting? What opportunities did you let pass you by?

2. Feel the weight of frustration and regret on your chest, knowing that now, you'll never have the chance to do them. What you wouldn't give to have another chance to change things, to go back, to try everything you dreamed of doing, saying, experiencing...

3. Open your eyes. Breathe. You're still alive. It's not too late. You have time to do everything you always dreamed of. Don't let a fear of failure stand in your way. Face your fears, take the risk and live the life you truly want.

Love yourself, now and forever

So, here we are!

How did it go? How do you feel?

I hope you enjoyed reading this book, and above all, I hope you've found it useful.

At the start of this book, I invited you to love yourself unconditionally. But that's easy to say and hard to do if you don't know how. That's why I committed to teaching you how to do it. To holding your hand throughout. I'm guessing some of my teachings will have been useful to you and others less so, some will have surprised you, others will have been revealing. The same thing with the exercises.

It's up to you from now on. All that's left for me to say is... CONGRATULATIONS!

I know that you have enormous potential. I know that you're sensitive, that you won't settle for a life without love, even if you don't express it in those words.

So many people talk about self-esteem, about loving yourself, about empathy and respect. Now, it's time to talk less and do more. You're already doing it. If only there were more people like you!

Love yourself. Remember all the things you've learned about how unfair it is not to love yourself. Don't live without your love, don't deprive yourself of it: you will be stronger with it, you will be happier.

Love yourself, and be the person you want to be. Don't try to do the opposite, don't wait to "be okay" in order to love yourself: it works the other way around!

I'll leave you now, but first I want to ask you for one last thing: for your self-love to be a source of inspiration to others. Let them forget about the happiness of success, and concentrate on the happiness of love.

Love yourself more!

Daniel

Your opinion is very important

As I'm an independent author, your opinion is so important to me and to future readers like you. I would be hugely grateful if you would leave me **a review on your favorite store** to tell me what you thought of my book **so that I can keep on improving it**:

- What did you like best?
- Is there anything you felt was missing
- Who would you recommend it to?
- ...

www.danieljmartin.es/review/lys

A gift just for you!

Would you like to **read my next book completely FREE**? Scan the code below and **join my readers' club!**

Great surprises await: be the first to read my new releases, listen to my audiobooks for free, get signed and dedicated copies... and much more!

www.danieljmartin.es/readersclub/

Other books by Daniel J. Martin